T0328697

Cambridge Elements ≡

Elements of Christianity and Science
edited by
Andrew Davison
University of Cambridge

EASTERN ORTHODOXY AND THE SCIENCE-THEOLOGY DIALOGUE

Christopher C. Knight
Institute for Orthodox Christian Studies, Cambridge

CAMBRIDGE
UNIVERSITY PRESS

CAMBRIDGE
UNIVERSITY PRESS

University Printing House, Cambridge CB2 8BS, United Kingdom

One Liberty Plaza, 20th Floor, New York, NY 10006, USA

477 Williamstown Road, Port Melbourne, VIC 3207, Australia

314–321, 3rd Floor, Plot 3, Splendor Forum, Jasola District Centre, New Delhi – 110025, India

103 Penang Road, #05–06/07, Visioncrest Commercial, Singapore 238467

Cambridge University Press is part of the University of Cambridge.

It furthers the University's mission by disseminating knowledge in the pursuit of education, learning, and research at the highest international levels of excellence.

www.cambridge.org
Information on this title: www.cambridge.org/9781009107761
DOI: 10.1017/9781009106009

First published 2022

A catalogue record for this publication is available from the British Library.

ISBN 978-1-009-10776-1 Paperback
ISSN 2634-3460 (online)
ISSN 2634-3452 (print)

Eastern Orthodoxy and the Science-Theology Dialogue

Elements of Christianity and Science

DOI: 10.1017/9781009106009
First published online: June 2022

Christopher C. Knight
Institute for Orthodox Christian Studies, Cambridge
Author for correspondence: Christopher C. Knight, fatherxopher@gmail.com

Abstract: This study examines the science-theology dialogue from the perspective of Eastern Orthodox Christianity and provides a critique of this dialogue based on six fundamental aspects of that theology: (1) its understanding of how philosophy may authentically be used in the theological task; (2) its understanding of the use and limitations of scientific and theological languages; (3) its understanding of the role of humanity in bringing God's purposes to fulfilment; (4) its sense that material entities should be understood less in materialist terms than in relation to the mind of God; (5) its Christological focus in understanding the concept of creation; and (6) its sense that the empirical world can be understood theologically only when the 'world to come' is taken fully into account. It is argued that Orthodoxy either provides an alternative pan-Christian vision to the currently predominant one or, at the very least, provides important new conceptual insights.

Keywords: Christianity, Eastern Orthodoxy, philosophy of religion, philosophical theology, science and religion

ISBNs: 9781009107761 (PB), 9781009106009 (OC)
ISSNs: 2634-3460 (online), 2634-3452 (print)

Contents

Introduction

The study of the relationship between science and theology is often referred to as the science-theology dialogue. My intention in this study is, from the perspective of Eastern Orthodox Christianity, to provide a critique of perspectives that have been dominant within this dialogue since 1966, the year in which Ian Barbour's *Issues in Science and Religion* set both the scene and the agenda for much of the mainstream discussion that has occurred since that time.[1]

While Barbour scrupulously outlined the perspectives of many modern theological traditions, a notable characteristic of the discussion he initiated has been a tendency to follow his own predilection for a rather abstract kind of theism. While most of the pre-eminent scholars in this field have been Christians, many of them have put little emphasis on the traditional doctrines that distinguish Christianity from other theistic traditions or on those aspects of the philosophical theology of the Christian world that have their roots in the pre-modern era.[2] This has meant that, except through their rejection of biblical fundamentalism, the majority of these scholars have not taken fully into account the ways in which specific Christian traditions might modify the positions they have developed.

In what follows, I shall illustrate the problematical nature of this approach by arguing that a number of topics that are important for the dialogue might be affected significantly if understandings to be found in the Eastern Orthodox community are taken seriously. A similar effect may perhaps be brought about if certain Western frameworks of a traditionalist kind are used in a comparable way, and certainly my hope is that my own critique will encourage others to use such frameworks to develop or expand comparable evaluations. However, while I shall mention such frameworks from time to time in what follows, I shall do so only in passing since my focus will be firmly on Orthodox perspectives.[3]

---

[1] Barbour, *Issues in Science and Religion*.

[2] Arguably, the dialogue in the late twentieth century was dominated by liberal protestant perspectives, sometimes – as in John Polkinghorne's work – shading into a more conservative protestant mould in which classical Christian doctrines are clearly affirmed but with little sense of their philosophical foundations and expansion. (For a comparison of Polkinghorne's work with that of Ian Barbour and Arthur Peacocke – who, together with him, dominated thinking in this field in that period – see Polkinghorne, *Scientists As Theologians*.) This situation is one in which thinking within the Roman Catholic world – such as that presented in John Haught's *God after Darwin* – has frequently been applauded but in practice undervalued. This situation may have arisen from the fact that some of the influential voices within the dialogue have been those of scientists with little theological training, while those who have had such training have often received it within traditions that put little emphasis on patristic and medieval developments of Christian thinking and focus primarily on supposedly 'biblical' perspectives and on the kind of modern philosophical discussion that largely ignores earlier philosophical perspectives.

[3] As my occasional mentions of it will indicate, an understanding that I regard as particularly promising in this respect is that of the 'return to the sources' or *nouvelle théologie* movement of the twentieth century, which – partly through encounters in Paris between French and Russian

It should perhaps be noted that, because an Orthodox consensus on science does not yet exist, the critique that I shall offer is based on *an* Eastern Orthodox approach, not *the* Eastern Orthodox approach. This is partly because Orthodox Christians, while unanimous in seeing the patristic witness as central to their theology, still often manifest a culpable disregard of Georges Florovsky's warning that to follow the Fathers means not simply 'to quote their sentences' but 'to acquire their *mind*'.[4] This insight has not been entirely ignored but – even when taken seriously – it has tended to lead to a rather narrow scholarly focus on understanding the patristic writers in the context of the era in which they lived. There has been little engagement with the associated question of how the patristic 'mind' might have implications for questions that have arisen only since that era. This has meant, among other things, that serious exploration of the theological implications of modern science has – at least until very recently – been undertaken by only a handful of Orthodox scholars, and no consensus position has yet emerged.

Indeed, in the work of these scholars we can find examples of all the attitudes to modern science that Barbour has categorized in terms of *conflict, independence, dialogue, and integration*.[5] In their details, however, none of these attitudes bear much resemblance to what in Barbour's terms would be their Western equivalents. This is partly because of the general distinctiveness of Orthodox theology, which means that the questions seen as relevant are often different ones.[6] It is also partly because Christian responses to science, in both medieval and more recent times, have not been the same in the Orthodox world as in the West.[7]

These factors need to be taken into account if we are to understand the way in which the Orthodox *conflict* viewpoint has not usually arisen, as it has among Western Christians, from biblical fundamentalism. Orthodox suspicion of science, where it does exist, has a distinctive historical and sociological

---

émigré theologians in the decades immediately after the Russian Revolution of 1917 – developed a reaction against neo-scholasticism and had a significant effect on the Second Vatican Council. For a varied set of studies of this movement, see Flynn and Murray, *Resourcement*.

[4] Florovsky, 'The Ethos of the Orthodox Church', 188.

[5] Barbour, *Religion in an Age of Science*, 1–30. There have been criticisms of this fourfold scheme but in the context in which I use it here it is sufficiently well known still to be useful as a 'broad brushstroke' framework.

[6] Ware, *The Orthodox Church*, has rightly observed (p. 9) that 'Christians in the West, both Roman and Reformed, generally start by asking the same questions, although they may disagree about the answers. In Orthodoxy, however, it is not merely the answers that are different – the questions themselves are not the same as in the West.'

[7] The only general study of this history in the Orthodox world is that in Nicolaidis, *Science and Eastern Orthodoxy*. The main developments examined in that book are summarized in Knight, *Science and the Christian Faith*, 37–44.

background.[8] Its attempts at theoretical justification do not arise from a belief in the literal inerrancy of the Bible but from a selective approach to patristic biblical interpretation.[9] However, most Orthodox scholars recognize that patristic writers often took the science of their own time very seriously, and in some cases anticipated aspects of modern scientific understanding.[10] As a result, this 'conflict' attitude is not common in the Orthodox scholarly world (though it remains so in the wider Orthodox community).

A more usual stance is the 'independence' position, in which it is assumed that science and theology do not interact. Just as with the conflict attitude, however, this view is not the result of the same influences as have given rise to a comparable attitude among theologians in the West. Sometimes, among Orthodox, it reflects little more than wishful thinking that science need not affect theological reflection because one can validly adopt something akin to the 'non-overlapping magisteria' concept developed – without much understanding of the nature of theology – by Stephen Jay Gould.[11] Sometimes it has been linked to the kind of postmodernist perspective that has been presented by writers such as Christos Yannaras.[12] Most frequently, however, it has been due to the influence of an older kind of phenomenology. Here, Alexei Nesteruk – from the perspective of one who (as a cosmologist) knows the sciences from the inside – has made a version of this position an influential one. He does not proclaim independence, as such, but stresses that science and theology do not interact in some abstract, impersonal way but can properly be understood only in relation to human subjectivity. Any mediation between the two pursuits lies only in the unity of the human experience.[13]

When examining work that corresponds to Barbour's other categories too, it is important to recognize the distinctiveness of the Orthodox versions of these attitudes towards how scientific and theological perspectives should interact. Though usually in a less complex way than that explored by Nesteruk, Orthodox scholars often implicitly assume the kind of 'unity of knowledge' that pushes the enquirer beyond the usual bounds of interdisciplinarity. This approach is sometimes described in terms of the concept of *transdisciplinarity*.[14] Often,

---

[8] Knight, *Science and the Christian Faith*, 37–45.

[9] An example of this selectivity is Rose, *Genesis, Creation, and Early Man*.

[10] For example, some patristic writers suggested a scenario that is distinctly reminiscent of evolutionary theory. See Till, 'Basil, Augustine, and the Doctrine of Creation's Functional Integrity'.

[11] Gould, 'Nonoverlapping Magisteria'.   [12] Yannaras, *Postmodern Metaphysics*.

[13] See, for example, Nesteruk, *The Universe As Communion*.

[14] The meaning of this term has been explored in Nicolescu, *Manifesto of Transdisciplinarity*. Its general meaning is, however, not tied to Nicolescu's particular approach. The term seems to have been first used by Jean Piaget in 1970 to advocate an approach to psychology that is not limited to recognizing the interactions or reciprocities between specialized fields of research. Rather, it

however, it is understood in terms of something on which I shall put great emphasis in what follows: the 'mystical' strand of Orthodox thinking in which Christian theology is – as Vladimir Lossky has put it – 'in the last resort always a means: a unity of knowledge subserving an end which transcends all knowledge'.[15]

The earliest Orthodox attitude in which the necessity of interaction between theology and modern science was recognized arose in the Russian religious philosophy of the nineteenth century. A significant figure here was Vladimir Soloviev, whose thinking was taken up in the early twentieth century by two of his more theologically mainstream successors, Pavel Florensky and Sergius Bulgakov. Relatively few Orthodox scholars of the present day have, however, been significantly influenced by these two. This is due partly to the fact that Florensky's death at the hands of the Soviets cut short his work, much of which has only recently become widely available, and partly to the way in which Bulgakov – who was exiled rather than killed – has often been considered idiosyncratic because of his way of focusing (as did Soloviev and Florensky) on the concept of divine Wisdom.[16]

Exceptions to this lack of influence can be found. Stoyan Tanev, for example, has been aware of their work in developing his analysis of ways in which the uses of the concept of energy in physics and in Orthodox theology might be mutually illuminating, while Gayle Woloschak has sometimes used insights from Bulgakov in her defence of neo-Darwinism.[17] Most Orthodox scholars who are active in exploring the impact of modern science on theology have, however, approached the dialogue from rather different directions.[18]

One such scholar is Basarab Nicolescu, who in the 1990s led the first major effort to develop a structured and widespread science-theology dialogue in a traditionally Orthodox country: his homeland of Romania. He has focused on the essentially philosophical issue of *transdisciplinarity*, attempting a significant (if arguably over-complex) explication of the 'unity of knowledge' outlook.[19] Another is Lazar Puhalo, a Canadian archbishop who, while not attempting any systematic analysis of the interaction between science and

---

locates these links inside a total system without stable boundaries between those fields. This understanding has now been expanded to incorporate the interaction of any two disciplines. Implicit in this approach is a more flexible attitude towards the accepted boundaries and methodology of each discipline than is usual in interdisciplinary work.

[15] Lossky, *The Mystical Theology of the Eastern Church*, 9.

[16] Bulgakov's sophiology has been used in an adapted form within the Western science-theology dialogue in Deane-Drummond, *Creation through Wisdom*.

[17] See Tanev, *Energy in Orthodox Theology and Physics*; Woloschak, *Faith, Science, Mystery*.

[18] A sense of the variety of approaches can be obtained by examining recently published anthologies of essays by different authors – see the 'Further Reading' section of the Bibliographies.

[19] Nicolescu, *Manifesto of Transdisciplinarity*.

theology, has written a number of short theological works that take up scientific perspectives in a way that is often full of insight.[20] A third is myself, whose work – on which the present study will focus – has its origins in direct participation in the science-theology dialogue that has taken place among Western scholars.[21] (This makes it particularly useful for presenting Orthodox insights to Western readers, as this study attempts to do.)

In my recent book, *Science and the Christian Faith*, I have already discussed some of the issues that I shall address in what follows.[22] However, that book was oriented towards the needs of ordinary Orthodox believers. This study, by contrast, is aimed at researchers and students who are interested in the science-theology dialogue as it has developed within the academic world. It focuses on the needs of those who already have at least a preliminary knowledge of that dialogue, whose dismissal of fundamentalism can be taken for granted, but whose knowledge of Orthodoxy may be slight.

In the light of the discussion I shall present, two things will, I hope, become clear. The first is that the Orthodox tradition has much to offer in developing an alternative pan-Christian vision to that which has become dominant within the science-theology dialogue. The second is that, even if this alternative vision is not judged to be preferable, Orthodoxy still provides, at a conceptual level, ways of looking at particular issues that may offer new and important insights.

1 Natural Theology

Natural theology has been defined by William Alston as 'the enterprise of providing support for religious beliefs by starting from premises that neither are nor presuppose any religious beliefs'.[23] Within the science-theology dialogue, this kind of natural theology has often been approached with caution, partly because of the failure, in the light of evolutionary theory, of its most well-known manifestation: the version of the argument from design developed by William Paley through the 'watchmaker' analogy set out in his 1802 book *Natural Theology*. This analogy is still often associated with theistic belief to such an extent that the insight that evolution may now be seen as the 'blind watchmaker' has become a significant component of atheist rhetoric.[24]

Natural theology is not, however, necessarily based on observation of the character of the empirical world, and it did not begin with such arguments but with others of a more purely philosophical kind. (The ontological argument of

---

[20] See, for example, Puhalo, *On the Neurobiology of Sin*.

[21] This is evident from my first two books: Knight, *Wrestling with the Divine* and Knight, *The God of Nature*.

[22] Knight, *Science and the Christian Faith*.   [23] Alston, *Perceiving God*, 289.

[24] See especially Dawkins, *The Blind Watchmaker*.

Anselm is a well-known example.) Over the centuries, these philosophical arguments were all challenged in one way or another, and by the middle of the twentieth century the resulting doubts about the possibility of natural theology were reinforced not only by the failure of Paley's watchmaker argument but also by the way in which logical positivism had made the entire project of philosophy of religion disreputable.[25]

This situation was changed in the second half of that century by the downfall of logical positivism within the philosophical community. This encouraged the development of a renewed belief in the application of straightforwardly 'logical' forms of philosophy to religious statements. In particular, the recently developed analytic form of philosophy seemed to some to be extremely promising in this respect.[26] As a result, interest in the philosophy of religion now seems to be focused at least partly on the kind of natural theology in which 'proof' or evidence-based 'probability' arguments for the existence of God have been attempted by philosophers such as William Alston and Richard Swinburne.[27] This interest has recently become influential within the Orthodox world, partly because of the influence of Swinburne, after his conversion to Orthodoxy in the 1990s, and partly because of a growing recognition that classical natural theology arguments were used in the Eastern patristic literature.[28] However, it is at least arguable that those who manifest this interest are not always sufficiently attentive to those aspects of the Orthodox tradition that have, over the last century, caused major Orthodox scholars – including Sergius Bulgakov, Vladimir Lossky, Christos Yannaras, and John Zizioulas – to 'view natural theology as at best religiously useless, in that it does not lead to a true knowledge of or encounter with God; and at worst as positively harmful'.[29]

A further point to note here is that those who try to develop 'proof' or 'probability' arguments for the reality of God tend to ignore the way in which the term *natural theology* is, in theological circles, now becoming understood in a broader way than it once was. When Alston himself spoke of it, he saw it much as the medieval scholastic tradition usually had: as providing support for religious beliefs independently of faith. However, not only was scholastic natural theology (as we shall see) sometimes more nuanced than is often recognized but recent historical overviews have made it clear that natural theology, as actually practised over the centuries, has often been more complex than definitions based on 'proof'

---

[25] See, for example, Ayer, *Language, Truth and Logic*.

[26] See the comments in Knight, "'Analytic' Natural Theology: Orthodox or Otherwise?'.

[27] See, for example, Alston, *Perceiving God*; Swinburne, *The Existence of God*.

[28] See the essays in Bradshaw and Swinburne, *Natural Theology in the Eastern Orthodox Tradition*.

[29] Bradshaw, 'Introduction', 3.

or 'probability' allow for, sometimes being closer in methodology to the kinds of approach advocated by modern Western theologians like Thomas Torrance and Alister McGrath, who explicitly argue that there should be no separation from faith or revelation of the kind presupposed in Alston's definition.[30]

Moreover, since modern approaches of the 'proof' or 'probability' kind are the result of strategies that are primarily those of scholars with a philosophical rather than a theological training, it is unsurprising that these scholars have sometimes been seen as insufficiently attentive to theological perspectives that urge caution towards such approaches. One of the most influential of these theological perspectives is associated with the understanding of Karl Barth, in which the possibility of natural theology was rejected. Early debates about this Barthian rejection were usually based on the contrary position taken up by Emil Brunner.[31] It was, however, probably the variation of the Barthian position developed by Thomas Torrance – articulated with at least some reference to scientific insights – that was most influential among participants in the science-theology dialogue of the late twentieth century.[32]

Torrance was an interesting scholar not only because of his use of scientific insights but also because he had a strong respect for patristic perspectives. Precisely how much his position on natural theology was due to this respect for these perspectives is perhaps not clear, but even if there was no straightforward causal link, his position does, if only partially, reflect patristic attitudes.

This consonance with patristic perspectives is exhibited by the way in which Torrance's later work embodied a distinct variation on earlier Barthian perspectives. The conclusion he eventually came to was that the problem identified by Barth lay not in natural theology per se but in the dominant Western version of it, which had been developed in medieval scholasticism and had claimed – though with subtleties that we shall note presently – to provide 'preambles of faith' (*praeambula fidei*).[33] He therefore came to argue not that natural theology cannot be valid but rather that it 'cannot be pursued in its traditional abstractive

---

[30] See, for example, Torrance, *Reality and Scientific Theology*; McGrath, *The Open Secret*. Russell Re Manning, in the 'Introduction' to his edited volume, *The Oxford Handbook of Natural Theology*, writes (p. 1) that one of the primary aims of that volume is to 'highlight the rich diversity of approaches to, and definitions of, natural theology. The lack of a fixed consensus on the definition of natural theology is due, in part, to its inherently interdisciplinary character and the inevitable limitations on definitions that belong firmly within particular disciplines.'

[31] For a brief summary of this debate, see Moore, 'Theological Critiques of Natural Theology'.

[32] See Torrance, *Reality and Scientific Theology*, in which it is argued that in its classic forms natural theology can be seen as inadequate in much the same way as Euclidean geometry can be seen as inadequate to describe physical reality in the context of Einstein's relativistic understanding.

[33] For a good modern discussion (more sympathetic to this concept than Torrance's), see McInerny, *Praeambulae fidei*.

form, as a prior conceptual system on its own, but must be brought within the body of positive theology and be pursued in indissoluble unity with it'.[34] In relation to arguments from the nature of the created order, for example, he insisted – as Alister McGrath has put it – that

> creation can only be held to 'reveal' God from the standpoint of faith. Nevertheless, to one who has responded to revelation (and thus who recognizes nature as God's creation, rather than an autonomous and self-created entity), the creation now has potential to point to the creator ...While the neutral observer of the natural cannot, according to Torrance, gain meaningful knowledge of God, another observer, aided by divine revelation, will come to very different conclusions.[35]

Torrance's stress on what can be known only through divine revelation in historical acts corresponds to one aspect of patristic understanding, as can be seen from the Cappadocian Fathers' way of stressing eschatological factors in their natural theology.[36] However, what is crucial for our comprehension of the Eastern patristic understanding is to recognize the importance it attributes to noetic perception, and here Torrance seems to have a blind spot that is arguably the result of his failure to challenge perspectives on the effects of 'fallen' human nature that have their origin in Augustinianism.[37] (In Torrance's own Calvinist tradition, these perspectives are often asserted in an extreme version.)[38]

The point here is that Augustinianism's influence was negligible in the Eastern part of the Christian world, so that the notion of 'ancestral sin' held by Orthodox is not the same as the Augustinian notion of 'original sin'. The image of God in humanity is not seen in Eastern Christian theology as having been so badly damaged as to have been effectively destroyed through human rebellion against God. For Orthodoxy, the created, 'natural' capacity to know God in an intuitive, contemplative way – though partially eclipsed in 'fallen'

---

[34] Torrance, *Reality and Scientific Theology*, 40.   [35] McGrath, *Thomas F. Torrance*, 192.

[36] See the comments in Knight, 'Natural Theology and the Eastern Orthodox Tradition'.

[37] It is arguable that the 'Augustinianism' of those who attempted to systematize the thinking of Augustine of Hippo after his lifetime failed to incorporate the full subtlety of his understanding into their own understanding. It was, however, their understanding, as much as Augustine's own, that affected Western theology's understanding of 'fallen' human nature so profoundly, and which was, in an even more extreme form, taken up in Calvinism.

[38] Calvin did affirm an intrinsic human 'sense of divinity' (*sensus divinitatis*) – which has become well known among philosophers of religion because of its importance for Alvin Plantinga's development of 'reformed epistemology' – but this is different from the Eastern patristic understanding of the inherent human capacity for knowing God. For Calvin, this capacity is viewed through the filter of his expansion of the Augustinian understanding of original sin in his notion of *utter depravity*. This depravity means, for Calvin, that although the *sensus divinitatis* exists as an aspect of our created being, there is no one in whom it 'ripens' (*Institutes of the Christian Religion*, 1.4.1) and it is, in fact, so corrupted in fallen humanity that 'by itself it produces only the worst fruit' (1.4.4).

human nature – has not been effectively obliterated in the way often assumed in the West.[39] (As Peter Harrison has shown, it was the supposed obliteration of the 'paradisal' contemplative capacity – particularly as expressed in Calvinism – that formed one of the main motivations for the justification that was often given in the early modern period for the scientific method.)[40]

In many Western traditions that have inherited an Augustinian understanding of the fallenness of human nature, the effects of this fallenness have been seen as applying less to discursive reasoning than to other human capacities. This means that philosophical thinking is used in these traditions as if its validity is independent of the spiritual state of the philosopher who uses it. The notion of the Fall prevalent in Eastern Christianity has, however, meant that its theology has tended, if anything, to move in the opposite direction, seeing the unaided human reason as potentially misleading because it inevitably bases arguments on presuppositions that require, for an assessment of their validity, a level of spiritual discrimination that may or may not be present. Its focus is, therefore, less on philosophical argument, as such, than on the spiritual discernment that is a necessary precondition for recognizing the validity or otherwise of these presuppositions.

One of the reasons for this Orthodox emphasis on something in human nature other than the discursive reasoning capacity is that its theology is characteristically an experiential one. Its approach is 'mystical' – not in the sense of being anti-rational but in the more complex sense in which it is stressed that Christian dogma, often appearing at first as 'an unfathomable mystery', is something that must be approached 'in such a fashion that instead of assimilating the mystery to our mode of understanding, we should, on the contrary, look for a profound change, an inner transformation of the spirit, enabling us to experience it mystically'.[41]

As we shall see in a different context in Section 2, an important aspect of this mystical theology is a radically *apophatic* attitude towards theological language, in which it is stressed that the words that we use of God can never circumscribe the reality to which they point. (This attitude – influential in Orthodoxy through the writings of the Cappadocian Fathers and of pseudo-Dionysius the Areopagite – has roots in Neoplatonic thinking. Because strands

---

[39] A variety of views is to be found within Orthodoxy, but even at its most pessimistic Orthodoxy is 'optimistic' by Augustinian or Calvinist standards, and at its most optimistic it reflects Justin Martyr's argument (1 Apology, 46) that even those who lived before the historical incarnation of the divine *Logos* could, through the love of wisdom, be sufficiently connected to that *Logos* to be, essentially, already Christian.

[40] Harrison, *The Fall of Man and the Foundations of Science.*

[41] Lossky, *The Mystical Theology of the Eastern Church*, 8.

of Islamic thinking have similar Neoplatonic roots, this apophaticism is to be found in the Islamic tradition too.)[42]

Related to this apophaticism is the concept of *antinomy*, which recognizes the importance of sometimes holding together concepts that can seem logically incompatible. (The Trinitarian notion of God's simultaneous three-ness and oneness is an obvious example of this.) In an important strand of Orthodox thinking, therefore, theology is not regarded as

> abstract, working through concepts, but contemplative: raising the mind to those realities which pass all understanding. This is why the dogmas of the Church often present themselves as antinomies ... It is not a question of suppressing the antinomy by adapting dogma to our understanding, but of change of heart and mind enabling us to attain to the contemplation of the reality which reveals itself to us as it raises us to God, and unites us, according to our several capacities, to Him.[43]

Behind this apophatic approach lies the way in which – in the Greek patristic understanding, and especially in its later use within the Byzantine hesychast tradition[44] – knowledge of God is far more than an understanding based on the discursive reasoning faculty. Such knowledge is, in this understanding, based first and foremost on contemplation (*theōria* in Greek) which is seen as the perception or vision of the highest human faculty, the 'intellect' (*nous*). This intellect is not the same as the discursive reasoning faculty (*dianoia*), which latter is understood as functioning properly in theological analysis only if rooted in the spiritual knowledge (*gnōsis*)[45] obtainable through the intellect.

According to this understanding, the intellect – when the darkening of its functions in 'fallen' humanity is overcome through divine grace – provides not knowledge *about* the creation but rather a *direct* apprehension or spiritual perception of the inner essences or principles (*logoi*) of the components of the cosmos created by the divine *Logos* (Word) and ultimately of that divine *Logos* itself. (As we shall see in Section 4, the intimate connection between the divine

---

[42] The Islamic aspect of the apophatic tradition is especially prominent in Shi'ite thinking. See the 'Shi'ite Doctrine' article in the online *Encyclopaedia Iranica*: www.iranicaonline.org/articles/shiite-doctrine.

[43] Lossky, *The Mystical Theology of the Eastern Church*, 43.

[44] This word *hesychast*, deriving from the Greek term for silence or stillness, refers to the understanding of contemplative practice which has – especially since its defence by Gregory Palamas in the fourteenth century – been dominant within Orthodoxy and in particular in its monastic practice.

[45] In the Orthodox understanding, this *gnōsis* is not the same as that which was at the heart of the heretical Gnosticism of the early Christian centuries, which was based on secret teachings. *Gnōsis*, in the Orthodox sense, represents a deeper understanding than is usual of the public teachings and practices of the church. For an explanation of this and the other terms used in this paragraph, see the glossary given in Palmer, Sherrard, and Ware, *The Philokalia*, 357–67.

Logos and the *logos* of each created thing is central to the Orthodox doctrine of creation.) This means that what is primarily needed in relation to the cosmos is not the kind of scientific or philosophical understanding available through the use of the discursive reasoning faculty alone (though such knowledge is by no means seen as irrelevant). What is essential is something quite different: the perception that arises from the kind of contemplation of nature (*theōria physikē*)[46] that is informed by asceticism and worship,[47] in which 'the same kind of noetic, contemplative deportment that Plato had reserved solely for the eternal forms, denuded of any earthly encumbrance, is now directed towards the cosmos itself'.[48]

In this understanding, it is usually assumed that because the perception of the *logoi* of created things must be *logikos* – logical in the sense of being in accordance with reason – the process of attaining this perception should not exclude the *dianoia* in an ordered co-operation of human perceptive faculties that is made possible by divine grace. However, the use of the discursive reasoning capacity to explore the things of God can only be authentic when that capacity is freed from the distortions that arise from the 'passions' and becomes, in a sense, more than human.[49] This means that the 'normal' reasoning capacity associated with our 'fallen' state is, on its own, inadequate for authentic contemplation of nature.[50]

These considerations suggest that purely philosophical approaches to natural theology fail to correspond fully to the kind of patristic methodology in which an intuitive element, fostered by the spiritual life, is central. A further consideration relies, however, not on a particular reading of the Christian tradition but on more abstract considerations, of the kind that philosophers working within the analytic tradition ought to be able to appreciate without recourse to wider

---

[46] A useful survey of Eastern patristic understandings of the contemplation of the natural world is given in Lollar, *To See into the Life of Things*.

[47] What David Bradshaw has said of science seems also, in this context, to be true of modern philosophy (including natural theology in its analytic form): that it has an orientation that is fundamentally 'anti-ascetic, in that it presupposes that there is no connection between one's ability to understand reality and one's moral character or the state of one's soul' (Bradshaw, 'The Logoi of Beings in Patristic Thought', 10).

[48] Foltz, *The Noetics of Nature*, 166.

[49] 'Passions' in this usage does not simply signify emotions but the kind of disordered appetites associated with the fallen state. It is the overcoming of this disordered state that is involved in the attainment of 'dispassion' (*apatheia*) which is central to the Orthodox understanding of spiritual progress. (See the comments on 'Dispassion' in Palmer, Sherrard, and Ware, *The Philokalia*, 358–9.) Evagrius Ponticus – often seen as the source of later Orthodox thinking about contemplation of nature – describes authentic contemplation as 'angelic'; see Foltz, *The Noetics of Nature*, 167.

[50] Patristic understanding is, admittedly, not uniform. For a discussion of this, and of particular examples in the patristic literature, see Knight, '"Analytic" Natural Theology: Orthodox or Otherwise?'.

theological perspectives. These relate to the philosophical question of what constitutes a persuasive argument.

This question is related to the way in which analytic arguments that claim to be persuasive of the probability of God's reality have not proved universally persuasive within the philosophical community – even to those of its members who are religious believers.[51] Indeed, some philosophers – equally well trained and equally as logical in their thinking as the scholars who are predominant in defending God's reality through their versions of the analytic philosophy of religion – believe that there are counterarguments that are persuasive of conclusions that are atheistic rather than theistic.[52]

When we ask why this can be the case, the answer seems to lie at least in part in the general observation that philosophical arguments defending theistic belief rely not only on logic but also on the *weight* that is assigned to various arguments and counterarguments. As John Hick has put it, the various attempts at evidence for and against the reality of God tend to 'fall naturally on one side of the balance sheet or the other'. Nevertheless, he goes on, we cannot conclude that 'one list outweighs the other ... For it would require us to quantify the values of the different items of evidence ... [and] any such quantifications could only be arbitrary and subjective.'[53] The important point that Hick makes here is that this judgement of *weight* is not – and cannot be – susceptible to purely logical analysis. It is something that relies at least partly on a kind of intuition. It is in practice only when one intuitively gives greater *weight* to one set of arguments and counterarguments than to the other that a judgement of their relative degrees of persuasiveness can be made.

In relation to this issue of the assignment of *weight*, what I have already said about the *nous* provides vital insights, since it allows us to go beyond Hick's pessimistic conclusions about the arbitrary and subjective nature of any such assignment. For, in patristic thinking, an intuitive faculty inevitably comes into play, and the objective component of this faculty is not equally operative in people who are in other respects entirely equal in conceptual knowledge and in reasoning ability.[54] The fallen nature of humanity is seen, in this traditional thinking, as having led to a diminution of the abilities of the *nous* that can be remedied only by divine grace through faith.

---

[51] For example, see Hick, *An Interpretation of Religion*.

[52] See Oppy, 'Arguments for Atheism', for a general overview of this issue.

[53] Hick, *An Interpretation of Religion*, 123.

[54] Intuition – as we experience it – has a non-objective component related to culture and personal experience. For this reason, it is not appropriate to rely on intuition without the spiritual training that makes true noetic perception its dominant component.

For all these reasons, while it would be wrong to deny that analytic arguments have any apologetic usefulness in a theological context, it seems necessary to deny the validity of the basic presupposition of any argument based on the notion that the question of the reality of God may be treated as a purely logical one. What is required in the use of such arguments is, from an Eastern patristic standpoint, more than innate reasoning ability that has been honed by rigorous philosophical training. Equally necessary, from this theological standpoint, are the qualities we refer to as sanctity and faith.[55]

Torrance once remarked that even the Western scholastic tradition once recognized an aspect of this insight since, as he puts it, for Thomas Aquinas it is only the 'baptized reason' that can properly engage in natural theology – that is, 'the reason endued with supernatural grace, for it is only as the reason is given knowledge of God that it acquires that adaptation by and through which it may think of Him and reason toward Him'.[56] This statement of Torrance's is, admittedly, potentially misleading, since Aquinas' work clearly affirms – in its *praeambula fidei* concept – the validity of at least some degree of discursive reasoning towards God that is independent of faith. There is, nevertheless, an ambiguity in Aquinas' understanding that Torrance perhaps has in mind in speaking in this way. This relates to the way in which, as Roberto di Ceglie has observed, God's influence on those with faith is, for Aquinas, such that they 'take the truths of faith as *orientation* and *criterion* for their rational enquiry, *orientation* because they aim to confirm by reason what they already believe, *criterion* because in case of a contradiction, reason must be considered as surely mistaken and rational investigation must start anew from the beginning'.[57] Moreover, the natural theology of Aquinas – usually thought of as the classic example of the *praeambula fidei* approach – is arguably only properly understood when we recognize that he not only practised both theology and natural theology but did so, as James Brent has put it, 'rather freely, and blended them into a *unified architectonic wisdom*. His architectonic contains both theology and natural theology (sometimes they are difficult to sort out).'[58]

Even if we take into account these subtleties in Aquinas' approach, however, it is necessary to note that, if we are to speak of 'baptized reason' in the context of the Orthodox understanding that I have presented, the term 'baptized' is, in this context, a metaphor for the effects of a kind of spiritual transformation. Its prime reference is not, as it is when applied to Aquinas, to the discursive

---

[55] As we shall note in Section 3, the patristic understanding of the relationship of faith to the *nous* is discussed in Laird, *Gregory of Nyssa and the Grasp of Faith*.

[56] Torrance, *Theological Science*, 104.

[57] di Ceglie, 'Faith, Reason and Charity in Thomas Aquinas's Thought', 143.

[58] Brent, 'Natural Theology'.

reasoning process. It is to what the Orthodox spiritual tradition often calls the heart (*kardia*). While Western understandings often see this term as referring to the seat of the emotions – and thus as having nothing to do with the mind – this is not the case in Orthodoxy or in the Greek patristic thinking on which its theology is based, in which an older biblical notion of the heart is still influential. The heart is, in these traditions, seen as the spiritual centre of our being, and its innermost aspect is nothing other than the *nous*.[59] One way of expressing this in Orthodox thinking is in terms of the way in which 'drawing the mind into the heart' is seen as a process that is central to the development of spiritual maturity and psychic wholeness.[60]

This understanding takes us beyond the stress on revelation in history that leads Torrance to insist that natural theology must be linked to a conceptually defined 'positive theology'. While such an insistence is, as we have noted, certainly to be found in the patristic literature, what is crucial to the Eastern patristic viewpoint is not conceptual understanding, of the kind that requires nothing more than philosophical training and ability, but the kind of noetic perception which – while sometimes partially expressible in conceptual terms – stresses that such terms are to be understood in a radically apophatic way. Without this noetic perception – which in its fullness is not part of our fallen nature but is a gift of grace – our use of concepts formed 'in accordance with the understanding and the judgement which are natural to us, basing ourselves on an intelligible representation', will at best 'create idols of God instead of revealing to us God Himself'.[61] (This is not, we should note, a view that is peculiar to Orthodoxy; the Reformed tradition's emphasis on what it often labels 'the noetic effects of sin' leads to similar conclusions, albeit in a way that is more pessimistic than Orthodoxy's in relation to the effects of the Fall.)[62]

In terms of the Orthodox emphasis on noetic perception, the way in which pro-theistic discursive arguments are able to lead to more valid conclusions than anti-theistic ones do is not to be understood in terms of a belief that the latter are less persuasive in terms of the criteria available to analytic philosophy. In terms of the perspectives I have outlined, it is because the people of religious faith who advocate pro-theistic arguments are those whose reason has been 'baptized' in the sense that, in these people, the *nous* has already been transformed from its fallen state in some degree, so that they are better able to assign due weight to pro-theistic arguments. They do not simply ignore reason (as those who take up

---

[59] This term 'innermost aspect of the heart' is given in the brief description of 'Intellect' (*nous*) in the glossary of Palmer, Sherrard, and Ware, *The Philokalia,* 361, in which reference is made to Diadochos of Photiki.

[60] See Bradshaw, 'The Mind and the Heart in Christian East and West'.   [61] Ibid., 33.

[62] See, for example, Moroney, *The Noetic Effects of Sin.*

a fideistic position do) but in their use of reason they implicitly challenge Hick's notion of the impossibility of quantifying the weight of different items of evidence in a way that is other than 'arbitrary and subjective'. The challenge comes, however, not from reasoned argument of the kind that any analytic philosopher can appreciate but from a contemplatively rooted theological perspective that relates to a different level of knowledge or perception to that with which such philosophers deal. From this higher level, the conclusions of those who adhere to the theistic paradigm may be seen as *truly* logical, in the sense that they are in accordance with a contemplative perception of the divine *Logos*. As Alister McGrath has put it in his own, more limited proposal for a 'new vision' of natural theology, the 'divine light of the logos allows us to "see" the created order in the proper way, so that human limitations in discerning the divine might be overcome'.[63]

In relation to the science-theology dialogue, the perspective I have outlined reinforces the critical attitude towards natural theology that is often to be found within that dialogue. Late twentieth-century participants in this dialogue did, admittedly, often exhibit a yearning for an approach in which scientific insights could be used to argue for the reality of God in an apologetically fruitful way. Nevertheless, they were usually cautious about the way in which this yearning was expressed and tended to avoid suggesting that some scientific insight could straightforwardly provide an argument for God's reality. At most, they usually either argued, as Arthur Peacocke did, in terms of 'inference to the best explanation' or else, as John Polkinghorne did, in terms of a 'revived and revised natural theology' based on the way in which science 'seems to throw up questions which point beyond itself and transcend its power to answer'.[64] But even with these scholars, the historical precedent of the Darwinian demolition of watchmaker arguments led them to adopt a cautious approach, and many of their colleagues in the science-theology dialogue were even more wary of pursuing arguments for the reality of God on the basis of scientific insights.

One reason for this wariness was that they tended to see their main role as that of developing a scientifically informed 'theology of nature'. This was seen as a central part of the 'dialogue' approach advocated by Ian Barbour, while natural theology (as usually then understood) was seen in terms of the kind of 'integration' attitude that he described but did not encourage. Theology of nature – as Barbour put it – 'does not start from science, as some versions of natural theology

---

[63] McGrath, *The Open Secret*, 173.

[64] Polkinghorne, *Science and Creation*, 15; cf. Peacocke, *Paths from Science towards God*. Polkinghorne did, however, later – in relation to anthropic considerations of the kind that we shall examine in Section 4 – suggest that such considerations, while not 'logically coercive', could be considered 'persuasive' of the reality of God (Polkinghorne, *Reason and Reality*, 80).

do. Instead, it starts from a religious tradition based on religious experience and historical revelation ... Here science and religion are considered to be relatively independent sources of ideas, but with some areas of overlap in their concerns.'[65]

Yet another factor that was often taken into account by members of that earlier generation of science-religion scholars arose from their interest in the philosophy of science,[66] which made them aware of how mid-twentieth-century developments in that branch of philosophy had affected the understanding not only of how rational argument functions within science but also of how, in a more general way, Thomas Kuhn's notion of scientific paradigms indicated the necessity of at least some degree of 'postmodernist' wariness of apparently logical arguments.[67] While only a few of them pursued the resulting postfoundationalist perspectives to any great extent, many recognized that an important modification to earlier understandings of the scope of rationality might be necessary.[68]

The focus on the noetic dimension of theological knowledge that I have outlined takes us, however, beyond the reservations about natural theology that have been expressed within the dialogue hitherto. This focus not only reinforces the importance of these reservations but points towards the relevance and importance of another aspect of the dialogue: that which relates to the nature of, and relationship between, the ways in which theological and scientific languages are used. It is to this topic, therefore, that we shall now turn.

2 The Languages of Science and Theology

A concept that has been important for the science-theology dialogue ever since Barbour's pioneering work is that of *critical realism*, which he saw as the proper way of interpreting the languages of both science and theology. Central to his understanding was the role of models and analogies in the use of both languages.[69] Scientific language, in his understanding, makes 'tentative ontological claims that there are entities in the world something like those postulated'[70] and in his view – and that of many of his successors within the

---

[65] Barbour, *Religion in an Age of Science*, 26.

[66] See my discussion of these developments in Knight, *Wrestling with the Divine*, 49–55.

[67] Postmodernism as a whole was not, however, regarded sympathetically by most participants in the science-theology dialogue, since they were aware that many postmodernist assessments of science are remarkably inaccurate.

[68] See the comments in Knight, 'Natural Theology: Complementary Perspectives from the Science-Theology Dialogue and the Eastern Orthodox Tradition'. For an example of pursuing postfoundationalist perspectives, see van Huyssteen, 'Postfoundationalism in Theology and Science'.

[69] Barbour, *Issues in Science and Religion*, 156–74, 216–18.

[70] Barbour, *Religion in an Age of Science*, 43.

dialogue – theology, though with greater reservations, can be said to do the same.

This kind of realism is 'critical' in the sense that it recognizes the way in which, in the history of science, changes in what was held to be the ontology of the world have sometimes occurred, so that we must reject the naïve realism often held in the nineteenth century, which assumed an exact correspondence between the entities postulated by scientific theory and the entities actually existing in the world. This critical realism has, however, often been interpreted by participants in the science-theology dialogue in terms of Karl Popper's sense of 'increasing verisimilitude' in the development of scientific theory. In a way that arguably oversimplifies what Popper himself claimed, many of them have taken their bearings from his understanding by presuming that scientific theory truly points to what the world consists of – to its ontology – and that successive theories do so ever more accurately.

There are a number of problems associated with this understanding, which have been debated by philosophers but largely ignored by the dialogue's participants.[71] One of these problems is that scientific theory changes sometimes involve major changes in ontological description, which are hard to see as consonant with the notion of increasing ontological verisimilitude. Moreover, as Thomas Kuhn has noted, in two successive changes there may not even be a continuous direction of change. Kuhn, on the basis of this and other considerations, took up a sceptical stance in relation to scientific realism, especially in its ontologically focused form, declaring that 'the notion of a match between the ontology of a theory and its "real" counterpart in nature now seems to me illusive in principle'.[72] This stance has sometimes been interpreted as 'anti-realist' but this may be a simplistic interpretation of his views.[73] In general, certainly, anti-realism has not been widely accepted among philosophers of science. Working scientists usually feel instinctively that their theories genuinely point to the way the world really is, and the majority of philosophers would agree that, unless this were the case, the extraordinary success of the sciences – practical as well as theoretical – would be inexplicable.[74]

Some of these philosophers have, however, suggested that a coherent scientific realism should cease focusing on the ontology of entities. Mary Hesse, for example, in her understanding of physics, has argued for what she calls

---

[71] For a recent examination of philosophers' discussions of this topic, see Oddie, 'Truthlikeness'.

[72] Kuhn, *The Structure of Scientific Revolutions*, 206–7.

[73] See section 7 ('Historical Challenges to Scientific Realism') in Liston, 'Scientific Realism and Antirealism'.

[74] For an account of recent philosophical debate on this issue, see Liston 'Scientific Realism and Antirealism'.

structural realism. It is, she says, 'undeniable that mathematical structures become ever more unified and universal with every advance in theory; the structural realm of physics is truly progressive'. However, she observes, 'the substantial description of what the structures relate changes radically from theory to theory'.[75] We should, she suggests, be realists about the structures that science claims to reveal but not about the ontology that is assumed in the description and investigation of these structures.

A comparable understanding arises from the work of Rom Harré on what he calls *referential realism*, in which two modes of scientific reference are distinguished. The first – as in the statement 'this grey powder is a sample of gallium' – requires, as he puts it, simply the ability to 'pick out a figure from a ground'. The second – as in the statement 'whatever is the cause of these bubbles is a neutrino' – involves the cognitive act of conceiving and accepting a theoretical account of the possible causes of an observed phenomenon.[76] The importance of this distinction, he suggests, is that the latter mode of reference – which he regards as being as legitimate as the first – is in practice often uncritically translated by scientists into the first kind of referential statement through an essentially arbitrary ontological assumption. He gives the example of the neutrino and the cloud chamber bubbles that first revealed its existence. There is, he argues, nothing in the formal referential statement – 'whatever is the cause of these bubbles is a neutrino' – that makes it necessary to conceive the neutrino as it is usually conceived: as a particle. (Indeed, he notes, there exists an alternative metaphysics in the understanding advocated by the quantum physicist David Bohm.)[77] 'The logical grammar of the ... referential format', Harré argues, 'is neutral. It is the conservative metaphysical predilections of physicists [in this case their quasi-instinctive tendency to think in terms of "particles"] that push the ontology that way.'[78]

Arguments of this kind – for some reinforced by the notion of 'ontological relativity' developed by W. V. Quine[79] – suggest that we should be wary of accepting the ontologically focused kind of critical realism that many participants in the science-theology dialogue speak of as a proper interpretation of the status of scientific theory. However, this justifiable wariness should not be taken to imply that it is not possible to defend the referential success of scientific theory. Rather, it suggests that a kind of radically modified critical realism – abandoning even 'tentative' claims about ontology and in their place positing valid *reference* – might be the best way forward in the debate about the nature of scientific understanding. According to this modified understanding of scientific

---

[75] Hesse, 'Physics, Philosophy and Myth', 188.   [76] Harré, *Varieties of Realism*, 75–76.
[77] Bohm, *Wholeness and the Implicate Order*.   [78] Harré, *Varieties of Realism*, 316.
[79] Quine, 'Ontological Relativity'.

critical realism, we can legitimately explore the structure of the world and validly *refer* to aspects of that world but at the same time must be extremely wary of thinking that we have a grasp of the world's ontology.

Many participants in the science-theology dialogue – following Barbour's notion of the parallels between theological and scientific rationality – have seen scientific critical realism as having implications for how we should understand the realism of theological language. However, they rarely acknowledge the kind of modification to scientific critical realism that the work of philosophers such as Hesse and Harré suggests is necessary and therefore fail to see how this modification, if applied to theological as well as to scientific language, may be important in reinforcing a view of theological language that is characteristic of Orthodoxy.

Particularly in the form of it expounded by people like Vladimir Lossky, this Orthodox view of theological language manifests a different understanding to any to be found in Western theological traditions. This view is rooted in a number of patristic writings, which distinguish two possible theological paths: that of *cataphatic* or positive theology, which proceeds by affirmations, and that of *apophatic* or negative theology, which proceeds by negations. Lossky notes that in Western theology these two ways – even when acknowledged – tend in practice to be reduced to one, simply making negative theology a corrective to affirmative theology.[80] The Orthodox understanding, Lossky suggests, tends to have a different and more radical understanding of the importance of apophaticism, so that cataphatic affirmations are seen primarily as providing a kind of ladder towards an increasingly contemplative and non-conceptual knowledge of God.[81] This understanding is, he notes, based in part on the kind of approach evident in Gregory of Nyssa, for whom the concepts we form 'in accordance with the understanding and the judgement which are natural to us, basing ourselves on an intelligible representation, create idols of God instead of revealing to us God Himself'.[82]

Lossky insists, for example, that the terms that we apply to God in cataphatic theology are not 'rational notions which we formulate, the concepts with which our intellect constructs a positive science of the divine nature'. Rather, he says, they are 'images or ideas intended to guide us and fit our faculties for the

---

[80] This Western acknowledgement is clear, for example, in those strands of the medieval Western thinking that were influenced by the writings attributed to Dionysius the Areopagite, particularly after a translation of those writings into Latin (produced by John Scotus Eriugena in 862) became influential in the twelfth century. However, in later thinking there was a tendency to treat 'mystical theology' as a specialized 'branch' of theology rather than as what Lossky urges: the overarching context for all theology.

[81] Lossky, *The Mystical Theology of the Eastern Church*, 40.   [82] Ibid., 33.

contemplation of that which passes all understanding'.[83] (This view is comparable to that of an exponent of the *nouvelle théologie* in the West, Yves Congar,
who stresses that what we can know about God does not constitute objective
knowledge of an abstract kind but is to be understood in soteriological terms
related to our human condition.)[84]

Sometimes, the radical apophaticism of Orthodox theological writers is
expressed by them only in terms of the recognition that we cannot straightforwardly apply to God categories comprehended in relation to created things.
However, in the patristic period, apophaticism was sometimes understood more
broadly. For Basil the Great, in particular, it was (as Lossky notes) 'not the
divine essence alone but also created essences that could not be expressed in
concepts. In contemplating any object we analyse its properties; it is this which
enables us to form concepts. But this analysis can in no case exhaust the content
of the object of perception.' There will always remain a kind of 'residue, which
escapes analysis and which cannot be expressed in concepts, it is the unknowable depth of things, that which constitutes their true, indefinable essence'.[85]

Over and above the modern philosophical arguments about the ontology of
created things that I have outlined, this Basilian view challenges the simplistic
critical realism that is characteristic of the science-theology dialogue by
pointing towards what we might call *apophatic critical realism*, which acknow-
ledges that, while we can validly *refer* to both God and created things, there are
aspects of both that are unknowable by us in conceptual terms, so that we must
be extremely wary of thinking that our words can ever circumscribe their reality.

This apophatic aspect of critical realism has not, we should perhaps note,
been entirely absent from the science-theology dialogue. In my own work it has
been seen as important,[86] while among Western scholars it has perhaps been
Arthur Peacocke who has been most aware that models in both science and
theology 'are concerned less with picturing objects than with depicting

---

[83] Ibid., 40. This focus on theological language as providing a contemplative ladder towards a non-
conceptual knowledge of God is comparable to that to be found in the work of another Orthodox
writer, Philip Sherrard, who – defending a kind of religious pluralism – has stressed the way in
which God's revelation of Himself is both oriented towards and limited by our human condition.
See Sherrard, *Christianity*.

[84] Congar stresses that God is known through what he calls 'signs' which are always oriented
primarily towards salvation, being 'proportionate to the human condition' and couched 'in the
language of men, in images, concepts and judgments like our own' (quoted in Henn, 'The
Hierarchy of Truths According to Yves Congar. O.P.', 115). Congar sees the content of these
signs as having a genuine ontological content but this must, he insists, be expressed in terms of
'mysteries' – partially hidden truths – made present most fully in the liturgical celebration of
salvation and always, when expressed linguistically, to be approached apophatically.

[85] Lossky, *The Mystical Theology of the Eastern Church*, 33.

[86] Knight, *Wrestling with the Divine*, 97–105.

processes, relations and structures (i.e. patterns of relationship). What matter is "in itself" and what God is "in himself" are left as unknown and unknowable.'[87]

Here, the work of Janet Martin Soskice seems to have had a strong influence on Peacocke's thinking, leading him away from a simplistic focus on the ontology of entities and towards the importance of the concept of *reference*.[88] What Soskice perceptively analyses is the way in which religious language usage can be clarified in terms of the theory of reference developed (in a non-theological context) by philosophers such as Hilary Putnam and Saul Kripke.[89] She focuses, in particular, on Kripke's concept of an initial 'dubbing event', applying this concept to mystical experience, which (for those in theistic traditions) will have led to the dubbing event that 'whatever caused this experience is God'. The Christian mystic, she notes, is in fact 'of all theists the most likely to be a realist, aware of the presence and reality of God, yet aware at the same time of the inability of human speech and thought to contain him'.[90]

However, as I have discussed elsewhere, while Soskice makes some important observations about the concepts of 'real essences' and 'natural kinds' used within the philosophical theory of reference that she adopts, both she and Peacocke fail to develop fully their embryonic insights into the kind of *apophatic critical realism* in which – as for Basil the Great – there will always be something about both God and created things that escapes analysis and cannot be expressed in concepts.[91] In relation to created things, one aspect of this 'escape' is – as we shall see in Section 3 – the avoidance, in Orthodox thinking, of the kind of materialism that views the real essence of a physical substance in the way that Kripke does: in terms of its chemical composition. Rather, this composition is, for an important component of Orthodox understanding, no more than an 'outward' aspect of what that substance is in the 'mind of God'.

3 Body, Mind, and the 'Mind of God'

For the scientist, the human being is the most complex part of the universe known to us, with mental and creative capacities continuous with – but far more extensive than – those known in other creatures. In this sense, while humanity's central geographical position in the cosmos disappeared with the downfall of

---

[87] Peacocke, *Intimations of Reality*, 42.
[88] Soskice, *Metaphor and Religious Language*. (Peacocke's reference was, however, to her doctoral thesis since this book – based on that thesis – had not yet been published at the time of his own *Intimations of Reality*.)
[89] For an introduction to this approach, see Schwartz, *Naming, Necessity, and Natural Kinds*.
[90] Soskice, *Metaphor and Religious Language*, 152n206.
[91] Knight, *Wrestling with the Divine*, 97–105. For a discussion of real essences and natural kinds from a philosophical perspective, see Bird and Tobin, 'Natural Kinds'.

the geocentric model of the universe, its centrality in terms of complexity undoubtedly remains.[92]

For the Christian theologian, this scientific picture makes perfect sense, since the creation accounts in the Book of Genesis see humanity as the culmination of God's act of creation. This understanding has been particularly characteristic of Orthodox theology, not least because of an aspect of its anthropology which I have explored in more detail elsewhere: the notion of humans as mediators between God and other created things, sometimes expressed in modern times in terms of the concept of humans as 'priests of creation'.[93]

In this section, I shall, however, focus on another aspect of the Orthodox sense of what it is to be human, which interacts with scientific and theological considerations in an even more profound (and perhaps connected) way. This aspect of Orthodox thinking may be approached by considering the important question of how the various understandings of the term *soul* relate to current scientific insights into the embodied character of human mental functioning.

Within the science-theology dialogue, an emphasis on these scientific insights – which have arisen from both brain scanning and the study of the effects of brain damage – has been of considerable importance through its way of underlining the difficulty of maintaining the kind of body-mind dualism associated with Descartes.[94] In this theological exploration, there has, however, been little or no consideration of unconscious or intuitive processes, whether of the kind often hypothesized in therapeutic practice[95] or of the kind on which this section will focus: that which in early Christian theology was often expressed in terms of the ancient Greek philosophical concept of the *nous*.

This term *nous*, as we have noted in Section 2, is usually translated into English as *intellect*. In traditional Christian thinking, however, it refers to something different in character from what is usually now understood by that word. The intellect is not, for this traditional understanding, the discursive reasoning faculty. Rather, it is the direct intuitive faculty that is necessary for understanding what is true or real. In a religious context, the *nous* has often been

---

[92] Potentially this understanding of human exceptionality could be challenged by a successful outcome to the search for extraterrestrial intelligence. Arguably, however, this would simply expand our theological (as opposed to biological) understanding of the term 'humanity', in which it is the possibility of a particular sort of relationship to God that is central. Such an outcome would not, therefore, necessarily challenge the main perspectives set out in this section. See Knight, 'Astrobiology and Theology: Uneasy Partners?'.

[93] Knight, *Science and the Christian Faith*, 113–17.

[94] The most extended (if controversial) attempt to analyse these insights theologically is that set out in Newberg, *Principles of Neurotheology*.

[95] Uleman, 'Introduction', 5, has noted that Freudian or Jungian understandings have usually been rejected in academic or scientific circles as 'largely unfalsifiable'. In theology, however, they retain a certain influence, albeit rarely without modification.

seen as the organ of contemplation, the source of true wisdom: the point at which the human mind is in some sense in direct contact with the divine mind. Particularly in Christian theology, however, it has been seen – as in the work of Gregory of Nyssa – as having been diminished in its abilities by the Fall, so that the spiritual journey in this life is understood as one of increasingly returning the *nous* to its prelapsarian capabilities.

At one level, Gregory's framework manifests very clear parallels with that to be found in the Neoplatonic thinking of Plotinus about the role of the *nous* in spiritual development. As Martin Laird has observed, both Gregory and Plotinus employ the Platonic motif of the mind's ascent to the Incomprehensible, placing a distinct faculty of union at the apex of this ascent. This summit is seen as being reached only through a process in which the discursive reasoning ability eventually gives way to the direct contemplation that is the function of the *nous*. (As Plotinus puts it, 'we put aside all learning', or as Gregory puts it, 'every form of comprehension' is abandoned.)[96] A significant difference between Plotinus and Gregory is, however, that this ascent is seen by Gregory not only in terms of Plotinus' Neoplatonic under-standing of the *nous* but also in terms of the central Christian concept of *faith*. As Laird puts it, Gregory ascribes to faith 'qualities which Neoplatonism would reserve for the crest of the wave of *nous*'.[97] He goes beyond Neoplatonic understanding to stress *relationship* with God, emphasizing the 'sacramental origin and development of faith as well as the transforming character of divine union'.[98] There was, in Gregory's understanding, both a focus on explicitly Christian concepts and a very clear link between the experience of religious faith and those aspects of the ordinary functioning of the mind that were seen by his non-Christian contemporaries as having their origin in the capacities of the *nous*.

We may, of course, judge that we now need a different way of expressing these capacities. Nevertheless Gregory's use of the notion of the *nous* – still influential in the Eastern Orthodox community – suggests that some comparable concept may be able to provide for Christians a basis for combatting reduction-ism in relation to the link between mental functioning and religious faith. Even if only for this reason, therefore, the concept seems worthy of consideration.

Combatting reductionism has been a major preoccupation of the science-theology dialogue of recent decades, and the philosophical notion of *emergence* has been a central one in undertaking this task.[99] This notion has been applied, however, less to refute the reductionist attempt to reduce religious faith to

---

[96] Laird, *Gregory of Nyssa and the Grasp of Faith*, 127.   [97] Ibid., 2.   [98] Ibid., 128.
[99] The current state of debate about emergence is well represented in the essays in Clayton and Davies, *The Re-emergence of Emergence*.

psychology than to refute the attempt to reduce psychology itself to chemical and electrical processes in the brain. In this latter context, the reality of mental experience has frequently been defended by insisting that 'bottom up' causality – the only causality acknowledged in reductionist analysis – must be seen as being supplemented by 'top down' causal effects, so that the relationship between mind and brain is seen in terms of complex feedback loops. According to this view, the qualities often associated with the term *soul* – discursive thought, the sense of free will, and so on – are not simply to be dismissed as epiphenomena with no ultimate reality.

However, what is often dismissed in this analysis is the dualistic notion that these qualities can exist apart from the body. The result has been that the dualistic notion of the *soul* as a distinct entity has often, in recent thinking, been replaced by an understanding that is summed up in Warren Brown's term, *embodied soulishness*.[100] Brown himself developed this phrase in terms of his own focus on emergentism in the 'nonreductive physicalism' that he has posited in terms of the philosophical understanding of Nancey Murphy.[101] However, it can also be related to the 'dual-aspect monism' advocated by people like John Polkinghorne, which – without denying the insights of emergence theory – views the mental and the physical as complementary modes of a single fundamental reality.

In part, this view arises from Polkinghorne's knowledge of quantum physics, the interpretation of which is difficult because of the apparent role of the observer in 'creating' physical reality. While astonishingly fruitful in making predictions at the subatomic level, this branch of physics has proved extremely difficult to interpret philosophically. It seems to suggest that the world, until observed, consists not of matter in a particular physical state but rather of multiple potentialities described by a wave function. Only one of these potentialities is actuated through the action of an observer, who is said to 'collapse the wave function'.[102] This understanding leads, however, to counter-intuitive situations, of the kind indicated in the famous paradox of Schrödinger's cat, which poses the question of how we are to understand the situation of a cat, put into a box that has been set up in such a way that there is a 50 per cent probability that the cat will die before the box is opened and the situation observed. Quantum mechanics suggests, counter-intuitively, that the cat is in fact in two states just before the box's opening: one in which it is dead and one in which it is

---

[100] See, for example, Brown and Strawn, *The Physical Nature of Christian Life.*
[101] Murphy, *Bodies and Souls, or Spirited Bodies?*
[102] This phrase is associated with the dominant 'Copenhagen interpretation' of quantum mechanics, though as we shall note this is not the only interpretation available.

alive. Only when the observation is made is one of these two potentialities brought into being.[103]

In the judgement of some, this philosophical problem of the role of the observer in quantum mechanics has only been dealt with in a coherent way through the notion of 'the implicate order' that David Bohm has offered.[104] The widespread rejection of Bohm's understanding by his fellow physicists – who often seem to prefer paradox (or an unfalsifiable 'many worlds' interpretation) to the notion that reality should be interpreted in a way that is not essentially materialist – is not due to its being incompatible with quantum mechanics, on which Bohm was an acknowledged expert.[105] It has been rejected at least in part, it would seem, because of its metaphysical framework, which is often regarded as a form of the dual-aspect monism advocated by various philosophers and taken up by Polkinghorne. (It is also sometimes seen as a variation of the related Jung–Pauli principle, in which insights from both C. G. Jung's psychology and Wolfgang Pauli's understanding of quantum physics are combined to produce a dual-aspect understanding of reality.)[106]

Polkinghorne admits that at this stage of our scientific understanding we can attempt nothing more than 'pre-Socratic flailing about' in relation to this issue.[107] Nevertheless, he has sometimes expressed his understanding of the way in which the mental and physical are related in terms of his particular understanding of the soul. This understanding is arguably of considerable importance since it goes far beyond the simplistic equation of soul and mind that arose in the early modern period, focusing instead on the notion of the soul as an 'information bearing pattern'. In this way, Polkinghorne affirms the reality of the soul in a way that is related to Aquinas' Aristotelian notion of the soul as the 'form' of the body. His own view, says Polkinghorne, can be seen as 'an antique notion in modern dress', even though it differs from this traditional understanding because of his belief that the 'pattern that is the soul will have a dynamic and developing character' as well as having an unchanging component, so that the soul must be seen as something that 'forms and grows'.[108] The soul is, for Polkinghorne, not naturally immortal but is in practice made so by the way in which the pattern is 'remembered' by God after an individual's death and is ultimately re-established in a resurrection body. (He has occasionally

---

[103] For an accessible description of this paradox, and a more general introduction to quantum mechanics, see Polkinghorne, *The Quantum World*.

[104] Bohm, *Wholeness and the Implicate Order*.

[105] For reasons sometimes offered for rejecting Bohm's understanding, see Goldstein, 'Bohmian Mechanics'.

[106] See Atmanspacher, 'The Pauli-Jung Conjecture and Its Relatives'.

[107] See, for example, Polkinghorne, *Beyond Science*, 69–71.

[108] Polkinghorne, 'The Person, the Soul, and Genetic Engineering', 595.

expressed this view in terms of what he calls 'a very crude and inadequate analogy', using the distinction between hardware and software in an electronic computer to describe the eschatological state in terms of the way in which 'the software running on our present hardware will be transferred to the hardware of the world to come'.)[109]

An important question about Polkinghorne's notion of the soul has, however, been raised by Keith Ward. Why, asks Ward, does Polkinghorne feel it so important to avoid what he has described as 'retreating into Bishop Berkeley's idealist castle'?[110] One reason, Ward suggests, may be a common misunderstanding of the views of Berkeley, who did not, says Ward, claim – as many think he did – that 'physical objects do not exist, and that everything is in human minds, so that the world disappears when humans are not looking at it'. To assume that Berkeley thought in this way is, he says, 'a complete misunderstanding'. Berkeley – in assuming that physical objects cannot exist without some perceiving mind – was, says Ward, essentially saying that 'if there is a physical world independent of humans, it must exist in the mind of God . . . though not exactly as it is perceived by humans'. This position, Ward observes, is certainly idealist in the sense that matter 'exists as the content of mental acts, and could not exist on its own'. Nevertheless, he goes on, this position 'is not very far, if it is any distance at all, from classical Christian theism', since the Christian believes that 'God who is not material, can exist without a material universe, but matter cannot exist without God. If God is anything like a mind – and God is said to know, to act, to have purposes and to be wise – then Christians must believe that mind can exist without matter.'[111]

Ward himself does not ignore the scientific evidence that leads people to speak of the emergence of human mental processes from the matter of the brain but nevertheless takes a more straightforwardly dualist view of the transition to the 'world to come' than Polkinghorne does. What the evidence for emergence entails – what Polkinghorne calls 'the psychosomatic integrity of human beings'[112] – may, claims Ward, preclude certain types of dualism but it does not require quite the kind of simplistic anti-dualism that Polkinghorne and many others seem to suppose it does. Ward points out – as Polkinghorne does also – that the traditional Christian eschatological hope (at least as usually interpreted) is for the continuing or re-established existence of our minds in a resurrection body, and this resurrection body will in some respects be discontinuous with the body of our present existence. Where he differs from Polkinghorne is in his use of this hope as an argument for a kind of dualism.

---

[109] Polkinghorne, *Science and Christian Belief*, 164.   [110] Polkinghorne, *One World*, 109.
[111] Ward, 'Bishop Berkeley's Castle', 127.   [112] Polkinghorne, *One World*, 91.

The Christian eschatological understanding, Ward argues, constitutes 'one reason why a dualistic view is so important, because it allows my mental properties to be transferred to a different form of embodiment' in the world to come. The only relevant form of close similarity here, he argues,

> is mental, not bodily. Embodiment may be essential to being fully human, but there are different forms of embodiment possible for the same person. It follows that my mental properties and capacities cannot be wholly dependent on the structure of this brain, since this brain will certainly cease to exist and will not simply be replicated in the world to come.[113]

Ward compares the view that arises from these arguments to the dual-aspect monism advocated by the philosopher John Searle, but he judges this form of monism to be ambiguous because 'it is consistent with the belief that matter is the real causal basis of mind'. Even if it is acknowledged that minds are different from brains, he argues, dual-aspect monism is not in itself incompatible with the view that 'minds cannot exist without the brains that give rise to them, and minds cannot simply be decoupled and transferred to other forms of embodiment'. Instead of permitting this ambiguity, Ward prefers to speak of *dual-aspect idealism,*

> which postulates that minds can exist without brains, can be transferred to other forms of embodiment, and indeed that matter exists primarily to enable certain sorts of mental properties to be expressed, so that in the end minds have causal and ontological priority over matter ... What matters is that matter has been created to enable minds to emerge and to exist, as natural parts of the cosmic process.[114]

When applied to the created order, we should note, this view seems little different from the dual-aspect monism spoken of by Searle and Polkinghorne. It is 'idealist' primarily in the sense that it clearly affirms the ontological priority of mind on the grounds that God exists as a kind of mind prior to, and independently of, the existence of anything material. In this sense, Ward is surely correct in seeing the theological inadequacy of any dual-aspect monism that is understood purely philosophically rather than theologically. However, it would seem that Polkinghorne himself – while trying to avoid any kind of dualism – was also attempting to move beyond these limitations, and this poses the question of whether his views and Ward's – both of which posit a dual-aspect understanding of the created order – can be brought closer together. I shall suggest in what follows that this is indeed possible if we take into account Orthodox insights, which permit us to avoid some of the problems of Ward's

---

[113] Ward, 'Bishop Berkeley's Castle', 130.

[114] Ibid. This view is expanded in more general philosophical terms in Ward, *More Than Matter.*

understanding while, at the same time, more clearly retaining the priority of the 'mind of God' than is evident in Polkinghorne's approach.

The point here is that, in attempting to develop his own dual-aspect understanding, Ward is attempting to develop an understanding comparable to that held by at least some Christians in the patristic period. A figure particularly relevant here is Gregory of Nyssa, whose thinking about the *nous* – as Joshua Schooping has shown – exhibits interesting parallels not only with Berkeleyan idealism but also with the thinking of the physicist David Bohm.[115] Gregory was not, of course, attempting to answer the same questions (arising from quantum mechanics) as those addressed by Bohm. He was concerned with a question much asked in his own time: that of how an immaterial principle, God, could create the material universe. As George Karamanolis puts it, Gregory's answer to this question was 'that the question itself is misguided, because the world is not material at all'. Rather, for Gregory, the world 'is constituted of reasons or qualities ... which are generated in the divine mind and are recognized in the human mind. This does not mean that Gregory denies the existence of material entities. All he denies is the independent existence to matter.'[116]

Gregory's understanding, Karamanolis explains, is based on the notion that what ultimately exists is a set of mental realities that relate to the qualities we perceive in created things. For Gregory, these exist – and always have existed – in God's mind. God, he says,

> established for the creation of beings all things through which matter is constituted: light, heavy, dense, rare, soft, resistant, humid, dry, cold, hot, colour, shape, outline, extension. All these are in themselves concepts [*ennioai*] and bare thoughts [*psila noēmata*]. None of them is matter on its own, but they become matter when they combine with each other.[117]

As Karamanolis notes, this focus on qualities is 'not an *ad hoc* answer to the question of the nature of matter but rather part of a fairly sophisticated theory that permeates Gregory's entire work'.[118] In some of his works, Gregory calls these qualities *logoi* – 'words' or logical principles. For Gregory,

> none of the things that pertains to the body on its own [is] a body, not shape, not colour, not weight, not extension, not size, nor any of the other things regarded as qualities, but each of them is a logos and their combination and unity with each other makes a body ... these qualities which complement the body are grasped by the intellect and not by sense perception.[119]

---

[115] Schooping, 'Touching the Mind of God'.
[116] Karamanolis, *The Philosophy of Early Christianity*, 106.   [117] Quoted in ibid., 102.
[118] Ibid., 102.   [119] Quoted in ibid., 104.

In this passage, Karamanolis observes,

> Gregory makes clear that bodies are intelligible to the extent that they are made up of intelligible entities, the qualities or *logoi*, which are hosted by the divine intellect but also by the human intellect. While creation of sensible, corporeal entities amounts to the combination of the *logoi* of God, we, humans, in turn get to know these entities by combining the logoi that make them up.[120]

This ancient philosophical framework does not, of course, have much appeal for many present-day Christians. However, we need to recognize that the theological thinking of Gregory – like that of all creative theologians in all periods – is inevitably expressed in terms of the philosophy of the writer's own time.[121] It is often only from the perspective of a later period that we can begin to make a distinction between what is central to what is being expressed – the 'spiritual instinct' so to speak[122] – and the philosophical framework and (sometimes flawed) reasoning through which that instinct has been expressed. The philosophical framework that Gregory adopted and adapted may for many have little appeal now, but the quasi-idealist spiritual instinct that he seems to want to express arguably remains an interesting one.

Do these theological insights move us towards the kind of dualism advocated by Ward? One might initially think so for two reasons. One is that there are clear resemblances between Gregory's understanding of reality and the much later understanding of George Berkeley, which has been defended by Ward and others as consonant with modern scientific perspectives.[123] (The early twentieth-century astrophysicists Arthur Eddington and James Jeans, for example, both advocated an idealist interpretation of reality, with Jeans famously saying that the universe 'looks more and more like a great thought that a great machine'.)[124] The second is that, even if human mental processes should, at one level, be seen as an emergent property of matter, they have some characteristics that do not straightforwardly fit into the usual emergentist and evolutionary frameworks. Our abstract mathematical ability, for example, has often been

---

[120] Ibid.

[121] In the context of science, Whitehead, *Science and the Modern World*, 49–50, has put it this way: that there exist 'fundamental assumptions' in any epoch and culture, which 'adherents of all the various systems within the epoch unconsciously presuppose . . . [since] no other way of putting things has ever occurred to them'.

[122] For discussion of this concept of 'spiritual instinct' in relation to the patristic witness, see Knight, *Science and the Christian Faith*, 64–6.

[123] Karamanolis himself actually sees more resemblances in certain respects to the perspectives of John Locke. However, other historians of philosophy have seen Gregory much more in terms of his anticipation of the Berkeleyan understanding. See, for example, the views expressed in Hibbs, 'Was Gregory of Nyssa a Berkeleyan Idealist?' and Hill, 'Gregory of Nyssa, Material Substance and Berkeleyan Idealism'.

[124] Jeans, *The Mysterious Universe*, 137.

seen as something that is difficult to fit into the framework provided by evolutionary psychology in its usual 'blind watchmaker' form, since that ability seems to go far beyond what could have contributed to the survival of our ancestors.[125] (This may be seen as indicating an affinity between the human mind and the mind of God in the way suggested by Polkinghorne's understanding of mathematics as pointing towards a noetic aspect of reality.)[126]

However, even though Ward's focus on the mind of God does suggest that something akin to what he calls 'dual-aspect idealism' may provide the best way forward in thinking about the relationship between matter, the human mind, and the 'mind of God', neither of these observations entail the adoption of Ward's particular kind of dualism. This can be seen by noting that, in his attempt to defend a view that is comparable to that of Gregory of Nyssa, Ward is not in complete accord with it. For example, the human mind was, in the patristic period, often understood in a more complex way than is to be found in Ward's use of the term *mind*, which seems to be essentially that used by dualist philosophers of the early modern period.[127] There is also another question about Ward's argument that arises from aspects of the thinking of the patristic era. For when speaking of the kind of mind that can, in theistic perspective, clearly exist without embodiment – God's mind – Ward seems to think that human minds are effectively identical to it in their nature if not in their capacities. It is true that there is, in this identification, something that reflects an aspect of the thinking of Gregory of Nyssa, for whom – as we have noted – the *logoi* of created things have their origin in the mind of God and are recognized by the human *nous*. Nevertheless, we need to interpret Gregory's understanding in terms of the apophatic attitude to be found in his own writings and in those of many others of his time, which made them averse to comparing God with

---

[125] This observation does not imply that an evolutionary framework must be abandoned, but it does suggest either some kind of 'guiding' of the evolutionary process or else some kind of framework in which the predictability of that framework is seen as part of God's initial design of the whole cosmos. The latter view is advocated in Section 5 of this Element.

[126] Polkinghorne, *Faith Science and Understanding*, 97–8. In a comparable way, the mathematician Roger Penrose, while avoiding any specific theological speculation, has argued that human mental functioning is non-algorithmic and that mathematics points to some kind of Platonic realm of reality; see Penrose, *The Emperor's New Mind*. In a related way, the sociologist Peter Berger, in his *A Rumour of Angels*, famously used mathematics as one of the 'signals of transcendence' that led him to take theological thinking seriously.

[127] As is often the case with philosophical defenders of idealism, Ward seems to work primarily with a somewhat abstract and pre-scientific notion of what the term *mind* might mean, with no basis in any kind of psychological data. The kind of patristic view that I have outlined, while certainly pre-scientific in the formal sense, was, by contrast, based at least partly on experiential data arising from spiritual experience and from observation of spiritual disciples by their mentors. The result was arguably a rather sophisticated set of psychological insights. An accessible account of terms used in the Eastern patristic tradition – and still used in modern Eastern Orthodoxy – is given (together with further references) in Vujisic, *The Art and Science of Healing the Soul*.

created things in any but the loosest metaphorical terms. Ward's rhetorical 'If God is anything like a mind' seems, in this context, very questionable.

These considerations suggest that, although Ward's arguments may validly be pointing us towards the need for a dual-aspect understanding that clearly incorporates the 'mind of God' in some way, his own attempt to meet that need may well be flawed. Admittedly, it remains to be seen whether a better approach could arise through other approaches, such as an attempt to combine Bohmian metaphysics with a revised interpretation of the *logoi* of created things, expressed in terms of inner essences and of the laws of nature so as to be more accessible to contemporary thinking. Whatever view we take of this possibility, however, one thing seems clear. This is that Ward is correct in believing that any framework for thinking about the concept of *mind* can hardly be adequate, from a theological perspective, if the origin of the universe in the mind of God is either effectively ignored, as in non-reductive physicalism, or else unexplored, as in Polkinghorne's version of dual-aspect monism.

One way forward in addressing this issue might be to attempt to 'update' Gregory of Nyssa's *nous*-centred approach in a way comparable to that in which Polkinghorne tries to 'update' Aquinas' view of the soul. A beginning to this process can perhaps be made by questioning the assumption – common to both Polkinghorne's and Ward's understandings – that, while the earthly body may be very significantly modified when it is transformed into a resurrection body, the earthly mind will continue much as it is in this life, differing only insofar as certain faculties, such as memory, may be made perfect rather than being (as at present) incomplete and fallible.

This assumption ignores two factors, one scientific and one theological. The scientific one is that most cognitive scientists no longer accept in any straightfor-ward way the analogy in which mental processes constitute the functioning of 'software' that will give the same results whatever the hardware that enables it to function. What we call the mind is, they increasingly stress, not only emergent from but also *conditioned by* the physical substrate with which it is associated.[128] This seems to be true not only in relation to the very specific way in which the brain works but also – if certain formulations of the notion of 'embodied cogni-tion' are accepted – in relation to the interactions between the mind and the rest of the body and between the mind and the world beyond the body.[129] If we accept

---

[128] This may be seen as an important factor in understanding why being fully human requires a body and not just a 'mind' of the sort that idealists sometimes envisage.

[129] Embodied Cognition is a growing research program in cognitive science that emphasizes the formative role the environment plays in the development of cognitive processes, based on a general theory that cognitive processes develop when a tightly coupled system emerges from real-time, goal-directed interactions between organisms and their environment. The nature of

these insights, then – unless the resurrection body and resurrection cosmos are assumed to be identical to those we experience in this life – the 'resurrection mind' that will be associated with the resurrection body and its environment will inevitably be rather different from our earthly mind.

The related theological issue here is that the Christian thinking of the early centuries did not always take the view that seems to be taken for granted in much recent theological discussion. Identity of our mental faculties before and after our transition from this world to the next was not simply assumed. As we shall see in more detail in Section 7, the Eastern patristic tradition often made a firm distinction between our present, biological state and the embodied state for which we were originally made and are ultimately destined. In this view, the 'original' and eschatological human state is something that has, in some sense, been 'covered up' by our present biological state – a view often expressed in the patristic period in terms of an allegorical interpretation of the biblical report that God gave 'garments of skin' to those expelled from Eden (Genesis 3:21).

A useful exploration of this aspect of patristic thinking is that of Panayiotis Nellas. He makes the interesting point that the patristic interpretation of our 'garments of skin' relates not only to the physical body but also to the soul, so that the term *garments of skin* refers to 'the entire postlapsarian psychosomatic clothing of the human person'. For writers like Gregory of Nyssa, he stresses, the Fall has brought about a situation in which the 'functions of the soul . . . have also become "corporeal" along with the body'. They form 'together with the body "the veil of the heart . . . the fleshy covering of the old man"'.[130] A corollary of this perspective would seem to be that, when the 'garments of skin' are thrown off in our eternal life, these functions will be transformed.

For many in our present era, the particular way in which this discontinuity between our present and eschatological states was perceived may seem unpersuasive. As we have already noted, however, the theological 'instinct' that lies behind early understandings may still be worthy of attention even when the particular way in which that instinct was expressed no longer seems to have any persuasive power. In this case, the need for attentiveness to that instinct arises from the scientific insight that human mental processes are not only inextricably linked to human bodies but also strongly conditioned by them. Given this strong conditioning, it seems to follow that a resurrection body that is significantly different from the earthly one – as assumed by both Ward and Polkinghorne – implies an associated mind that will be significantly different from that which we now possess.

---

these interactions, it is believed, influences the formation and further specifies the nature of the developing cognitive capacities. See Wilson and Foglia, 'Embodied Cognition'.

[130] Nellas, *Deification in Christ*, 50–1.

Related to this perception is another important insight that may perhaps inform our thinking about eternal life. This is the notion that what we nowadays tend to think of as constitutive of our minds and personalities – things like our discursive rational faculty and our memories – may in fact be no more than servants, in this world, of something more central to our being: the *nous*. The point here is that, in the kind of late antique and medieval Christian understanding that focused on the concept of the *nous*, our spiritual journey in this world was often seen as having as one of its prime aims the purification of that *nous*: the overcoming of the distortion or darkening of its functions in our present 'fallen' state. Often, in Christian literature, the *nous* was described as the 'eye' of the soul (*psyche*), and it was the full opening of this eye that was seen as making possible what is sometimes, in Western Christian theology, called the beatific vision.[131]

In the light of this understanding, it seems possible to understand the functioning of our 'resurrection minds' largely, or even completely, in terms of the transformed functioning of the *nous*. This suggests that the establishment of our resurrection minds may in fact involve shedding all that is other than the direct intuitive knowledge that arises from the perfected *nous*. (Something of this kind – albeit expressed in different terms – certainly seems to be hinted at in some of the most well-known New Testament passages that refer to our eschatological state.)[132]

Might it be, then, that those who are believers in the eschatological state should recognize that, in that state, we may not know *about* anything, or even 'think', in the sense in which we usually use that term? Rather – as Gregory of Nyssa puts it of our ascent to God in this life – 'every form of comprehension'[133] will have been abandoned, so that we will simply *know* – directly and intuitively – in the way that mystics, in their most sublime moments

---

[131] There are, we should note, significant differences between the way this vision is interpreted in Western and Eastern Christian traditions. See Constantine, *The Orthodox Doctrine of the Person*.

[132] In the Johannine literature, for example, there is a strong sense that eternal life is something that the believer can experience not only in the future but also now through knowledge of God. Indeed, in the fourth gospel there is the report that Jesus himself not only described but also *defined* eternal life as the state in which we 'know … the only true God and Jesus Christ' (John 14:3). In the Pauline strand of New Testament teaching the emphasis is, admittedly, different, with a stronger sense of eternal life as belonging to the future. There is also, however, a sense that we are unable in this life to anticipate what our eschatological state will be and that our knowledge in that state will not simply be an extension of the type of knowledge we have now but in some sense it will be knowledge in a mode akin to that of God's knowledge. What 'God has prepared for those who love him', says Paul, is something that 'no eye has seen, nor ear heard, nor the human heart conceived' (1 Corinthians 2:9). In this life 'we see in a mirror dimly', but in eternal life 'we will see face to face', knowing 'fully', even as we 'have been fully known' (1 Corinthians 13:12).

[133] Quoted in Laird, *Gregory of Nyssa and the Grasp of Faith*, 127.

in this life, are said to *know*. If this is valid, then continuity in our existence as unique *persons* will not necessarily involve the re-establishment of much with which we tend to identify ourselves. Rather, it may involve a transformation of our whole being that will be far more radical than we usually appreciate: a casting aside of our 'garments of skin' in both their physical and their mental dimensions.

In the perspective provided by this focus on the noetic aspect of our eschatological state, an important insight arises in relation to our use of the concept of the *emergence*, in this life, of our mental faculties from the matter of the brain. This is that there would seem to be no theological problem in seeing most aspects of our present mental functioning – those not intrinsically associated with the *nous* – as emergent properties of our biological bodies, which will cease to function when we die and need not resume their functioning when we receive our resurrection bodies. This permanent cessation of functioning may be seen simply as an aspect of the way in which the casting off of our 'garments of skin' at the material level involves also a casting off of all those 'functions of the soul' which, for Gregory of Nyssa and for other patristic writers, have 'become "corporeal" along with the body'.[134] In our eternal life, it may be that through the *nous* we shall simply *know*, directly and intuitively, in such a way that other kinds of mental functioning – at least in the forms in which we now experience them – will have become redundant.

4 Panentheism and Christology

One of the most interesting developments among science-religion scholars of the late twentieth century was a rise in interest in the concept of *panentheism*: the notion that the world is in some sense 'in God'.[135] (As we shall note in Section 5, much of this interest has arisen in the context of thinking about divine action.) Panentheism tends, however, to be defined by Western Christian scholars in purely negative terms: as a rejection of the notion – characteristic of traditional Western philosophical theism – that God and the world are totally separated.[136] Usually, in trying to explain what it is to be 'in' God, these scholars rely on some rather vague analogy, such as the relationship between the mind and the body or between a foetus and its mother. In terms of these

---

[134] Nellas, *Deification in Christ*, 50–1.

[135] This development was both reflected in and fostered by an influential collection of essays: Clayton and Peacocke, *In Whom We Live and Move and Have Our Being*.

[136] In the late medieval period, the predominant Western 'substance' metaphysics effectively forbade any kind of panentheism, while later attempts to move away from the resulting notion of separation tended to lead – as in the work of Spinoza – to a kind of *pantheism* in which the world and God were simply identified with one another. See the comments in Clayton, 'Panentheism in Metaphysical and Scientific Perspective'.

analogies, panentheism is in fact a position that takes many forms, some of which are mutually exclusive. We need, therefore, to be aware of this range of possible meanings and to recognize that, in its Orthodox form, panentheism is far more than simply the notion that the world is 'in God'. Orthodox panentheism arises not from a simple definition or analogy but from a subtle and profound theology of creation, which is very different from that usually held in the West since it explicitly rejects the characteristic tendency of Western theology to separate grace and nature (which was also questioned in the twentieth century by Western scholars associated with the *nouvelle théologie* movement).[137] As Vladimir Lossky has put it, Orthodoxy 'knows nothing of "pure nature" to which grace is added as a supernatural gift. For it, there is no natural or "normal" state, since grace is implied in the act of creation itself.'[138]

This Orthodox theology of creation has two main components. The first of these is expressed in terms of the concept (noted in Section 3) of the *logoi* – 'words' or principles – of created things. This concept was most fully developed in the seventh century by Maximus the Confessor.[139] As Kallistos Ware has put it, Maximus describes these *logoi* 'in two different ways, sometimes as created and sometimes as uncreated, depending upon the perspective in which they are viewed. They are created inasmuch as they inhere in the created world. But when regarded as God's presence in each thing – as divine "predetermination" or "preconception" concerning that thing – they are not created but uncreated.'[140]

This understanding derives from an understanding of the doctrine of the incarnation that is central to the Orthodox outlook but – despite increasing Western interest in Maximus in recent decades[141] – is different from that which remains common in the West. In Maximus' framework, the fourth gospel's assertion that the *Logos* (Word) of God 'became flesh' (John 1:14) is not seen

---

[137] See the interesting analysis in Swafford, *Nature and Grace*. It should be noted perhaps that the notion of 'pure' nature is not always seen as an intrinsic part of the Western tradition, though Henri de Lubac, from the perspectives of the *nouvelle théologie* movement, certainly saw it as an aspect of neo-scholasticism that required modification. (For an analysis, see Boersma, *Nouvelle Théologie and Sacramental Ontology*.) In classic Protestant theology, there was no formal sense of 'pure' nature, of the medieval kind, but the deism of the eighteenth century certainly assumed something comparable, and this had a widespread influence. Within the science-theology dialogue, certainly, an emphasis on the effective autonomy of the natural world reflects an understanding of a kind of 'pure' nature and this, as we shall see in Section 5, has led to a 'causal joint' view of divine action.

[138] Lossky, *The Mystical Theology of the Eastern Church*, 101.

[139] The Greek spelling *Maximos* is often used in texts aimed primarily at an Orthodox audience.

[140] Ware, 'God Immanent Yet Transcendent', 160.

[141] Significant studies of Maximus by Western authors include von Balthasar, *Cosmic Liturgy*; Thunberg, *Microcosm and Mediator*; and Blowers, *Maximus the Confessor*. These studies may be compared to recent studies by Orthodox authors such as Louth, *Maximus the Confessor* and Loudovikos, *A Eucharistic Ontology*.

simply as a statement about a historical event. Rather, Maximus develops his understanding through a subtle and profound perception of how everything was, in the beginning, created through this *Logos* (John 1:1–4). By moulding the philosophical categories available to him to the realities of the Christian revelation as he perceives them, Maximus expresses his faith in terms of the way in which the *Logos* of God is to be perceived, not only in the person of Jesus Christ but also in the 'words' (*logoi*) of all prophetic utterance and in the 'words' (*logoi*) that represent the underlying principles by which all created things have their being and act as they do.

The incarnation in Jesus Christ is thus seen not simply as a historical event, to be interpreted – as so often in Western Christian thinking – as a supernatural intrusion into the 'natural' order. Rather, what occurs in the person of Jesus is, for this strand of theology, intimately linked both to the whole history of the redemptive process and to the act of creation itself. It takes up the fourth gospel's insight that the incarnation involves – as one Western scholar has put it – not 'the sudden arrival of an otherwise absent Logos' but rather 'the completion of a process already begun in God's act of creation'.[142]

It is precisely this biblical insight that Maximus uses when he develops the *Logos* concept to describe a continuous process from the creation of the cosmos to the Christ event. Lars Thunberg's comment that Maximus envisages 'almost a gradual incarnation' may perhaps be imprecise in its terminology.[143] It points accurately, all the same, to an important aspect of Maximus' thought, in which he could go as far as to say (in *Ambiguum* 7) that 'the one Logos is the many logoi, and the many logoi are the one Logos'. This linkage means, according to Andrew Louth, that for Maximus everything in the universe 'has its own meaning in its own *logos*, or principle, but . . . all these *logoi* form a coherent whole, because they all participate in the one *Logos* of God'.[144]

Alongside this particular panentheistic model, in which the cosmos is viewed Christologically, there exists in Orthodox teaching another, which is more purely philosophical. This is to be found in embryonic form in the writings of Clement of Alexandria and Basil the Great but was developed most systematically in the fourteenth century by Gregory Palamas. This work makes a distinction between God's transcendent essence (*ousia*) and His immanent energies or operations (*energeiai*). This second approach, Ware says, is

> not contrary to the first but complementary . . . In his essence God is infinitely transcendent, utterly beyond all created being, beyond all participation from the human side. But in his energies – which are nothing less than God himself

---

[142] Need, 'Re-reading the Prologue', 403.   [143] Thunberg, *Man and the Cosmos*, 75.
[144] Louth, *Introducing Eastern Orthodoxy*, 42.

in action – God is inexhaustibly immanent, maintaining all things in being, animating them, making each of them a sacrament of his dynamic presence.[145]

Because of their explicit or (more often nowadays) implicit reliance in a 'substance' metaphysics, Western Christian scholars often see panentheism as inevitably tending towards pantheism: the identification of God and the world. It is important to recognize, therefore, that over and above the implications of these two complementary ways of expressing Orthodox panentheism, a third factor – which we shall look at in more detail in Section 7 – reinforces the anti-pantheistic aspect of this Orthodox panentheism. This is that there is often, in the patristic writings, a strong sense that the world we experience only partially reflects God's ultimate intentions for His creation. The eschatological state has, they suggest, more in common with the original state for which humanity was created (the Paradise of the Genesis story) than it does with the world that we now experience as 'fallen' beings. In a sense, they say, the whole cosmos now reflects the fallen human state.

In the context of the science-theology dialogue, there is an aspect of Maximus' understanding that is of great importance. This is his sense that, because the divine *Logos* is both the beginning and the end of all things – 'the alpha and the omega' as the Book of Revelation (21:6, 22:13) puts it – the *logoi* of created things should not be understood only as constituting the inner essences of those things (which we would now express in part in terms of the 'laws of nature' that they obey). In addition, for Maximus, the *logoi* must be seen in terms of the ultimate goal (*telos*) to which all created things are drawn. (Orthodoxy stresses that salvation has a cosmic dimension: it is not *from* the world but *of* the world.) The *logos* of each created thing is, as Kallistos Ware has put it, 'God's intention for that thing, its inner essence, which makes it distinctively itself and at the same time draws it towards the divine realm'.[146] Maximus' understanding is one in which, as Paul Blowers has explained, the *logoi* are 'principles or signatures of a creature's essence and nature, teleological "codes" that project creatures towards their fulfillment in the divine plan'.[147]

This teleological aspect of God's creation – in which the cosmos is 'dynamic ... tending always to its final end'[148] – has not often, however, been related by Orthodox scholars to scientific insights. One successful (if brief) attempt to do this, which echoes my own work on this topic, is that of

---

[145] Ware, 'God Immanent Yet Transcendent', 160.
[146] Ware, 'God Immanent Yet Transcendent', 160.
[147] Blowers, *Maximus the Confessor*, 113.
[148] Lossky, *The Mystical Theology of the Eastern Church*, 101.

Mark Chenoweth.[149] Another is that of Doru Costache, in which he contrasts the way in which science, 'epitomized by Darwinian evolution, does not mention the purposefulness of natural movement, whereas [Orthodox] theology … considers teleology crucial'.[150]

Costache's contrast between science and Orthodox theology is, however, potentially misleading. He is, of course, correct in this observation that modern scientific insights arise through a methodology that precludes any mention of purpose. However, what he perhaps fails to emphasize sufficiently is that the methodology of modern science *necessarily* avoids the concept of purpose.[151] What is important is not this avoidance but the way in which at least some scientific insights are susceptible to *theological interpretation* in terms of purpose, in a way that enables a teleological understanding to be seen as not competing with a scientific understanding. (As we shall see in Sections 5 and 6, this compatibility permits a view of divine action that is quite different from that usually adopted within the science-theology dialogue.)

There are two scientific insights that are open to teleological interpretation in this way. These are the 'fine-tuning' of the universe that is evident from astronomical evidence and the occurrence of 'convergent evolution' in the biological world. Both point to the way in which the role of chance in the development of the cosmos is not inconsistent with a broadly predictable outcome.

In the astrophysical arena, it has been known for several decades that the universe we live in seems to be 'finely tuned' for the emergence of living beings. There are a number of 'universal constants' – that which explains the strength of gravitational attraction, for example – which do not seem to have been constrained in any naturalistic way to have the magnitude that they have. Had these constants been only very slightly different in value, however, they would have precluded ours from being the kind of universe in which complex life forms could have emerged naturalistically. This kind of observation of fine-tuning has given rise to argument about what is sometimes called the *anthropic cosmological principle*.[152]

---

[149] Chenoweth, 'A Maximian Framework for Understanding Evolution'.

[150] Costache, 'The Orthodox Doctrine of Creation in the Age of Science', 54.

[151] Modern science arose historically from the insight that the teleological explanations of late medieval science actually provided less insight and predictive power than explanations based on mathematical laws of nature. It is for this reason that explanations would simply cease to be 'scientific' if purpose were posited as the only way to understand certain phenomena. (In practice, admittedly, certain phenomena can be understood in quasi-teleological ways, but these ways are seen by scientists simply as being a convenient kind of 'shorthand' for laws that may be understood in a more conventional, mathematical way.)

[152] Barrow and Tipler, *The Anthropic Cosmological Principle*.

In the biological sphere, a comparable view of the predictability of the interplay of chance and physical law has also recently emerged. At one time, there was widespread agreement among biologists that the termination of apparently promising evolutionary pathways indicated that the evolutionary process had no predictability. More recently, however, other biologists – the 'new atheist' Richard Dawkins among them – have pointed out that certain evolutionary pathways have been followed independently on a number of occasions.[153] In this sense, at least, the evolutionary process has a degree of predictability.

The strongest version of this latter perspective comes from Simon Conway Morris, who has emphasized the way in which certain adaptations to particular ecological niches have happened not only more than once but also sometimes from very different evolutionary starting points. For Conway Morris, this underlines the notion of *convergent evolution*, which suggests that a number of potential evolutionary pathways may, from very different starting points, tend to converge on the same adaptive features in similar ecological environments. (The resemblances in locomotive features between certain marine mammals and many types of fish constitute an obvious example.) Although he recognizes a significant degree of contingency in the evolutionary process, so that it is not predictable in detail, he nevertheless argues that, once life has begun in any part of the universe, something very like human beings as we know them are effectively bound to emerge naturalistically, though not necessarily through the kind of evolutionary pathway that our own ancestors took.[154]

In certain respects, this last speculation may be to take the validity of the notion of convergent evolution too far. Nevertheless, the concept of convergent evolution points us towards an important idea: that, to the extent that we see the biblical notion of humans being 'in the image of God' in terms of functional abilities in this world, it is possible to see the emergence of beings created in this image as something that can be coherently thought about in terms of the evolutionary interplay of chance and the laws of nature. (The only exception to this observation is, as we have noted in Section 3, what is traditionally described as the *nous*, since this is the aspect of our mental functioning that is, in Orthodox thinking, connected directly to the divine mind, and it relates not only to 'this world' but also to the 'world to come'.)[155]

These reflections on the effects of chance processes make it clear that we cannot simply interpret the role of such processes as signifying a 'meaningless'

---

[153] Dawkins, *The Ancestor's Tale*, 603–6.   [154] Conway Morris, *Life's Solution*.

[155] This understanding may perhaps be compatible with the view that, while evolution produces the animal aspect of human life, human 'souls' are an added extra. However, this view is arguably unnecessary in the context of the panentheistic and dual-aspect framework advocated here.

universe in the way that atheists are apt to do. The question inevitably arises, however, as to whether, unless these reflections are supplemented, they point towards a God who can be seen as anything more than the 'Supreme Being' of deism: the world's designer and initiator, who is now no more than an 'absentee landlord'. John Polkinghorne certainly saw this as a problem and sometimes perceived deistic undertones in the work of those of his Western colleagues who saw God's creative action purely in terms of the interplay between chance and physical law.[156] However, if Polkinghorne's criticism of this tendency is argu-ably valid in terms of his presupposition that God and the world are separated, what needs to be recognized here is that this presupposition is challenged by Orthodoxy's panentheism.

As we shall see in Section 5, it is the presupposition of a separation between God and the world – even when this assumption is formally repudiated – that leads the majority of participants in the Western science-theology dialogue to seek a scientifically literate way of describing a 'causal joint' between God and the world that 'allows' Him to act within that world, if not in relation to His creative action, then at least in relation to aspects of His providential action. The Orthodox doctrine of creation points, however, to a different understanding.

5 Divine Action

Once modern scientific insights had made clear that naturalistic processes can account adequately for most events in the world, a question arose for Western theologians: that of how divine action is to be understood. Their perception of this question was strongly influenced by their tendency to interpret scientific insights in terms of their understanding of the relative autonomy of 'nature', which had arisen from the 'clockwork' universe that Newtonian physics now seemed to posit (and which, for some, may have been reinforced by assumptions rooted in either the Protestant focus on grace or the interpretation of medieval philosophy in which a kind of 'pure' nature was often assumed).[157]

These developments meant that the natural world was now widely seen as one in which God – its designer and creator – was usually no more than an observer of its autonomous workings. The only way in which God could act directly was, it seemed, by temporarily suspending natural laws and then intervening in a 'supernatural' manner. Thinking about divine action was thus focused on

---

[156] Polkinghorne, *Science and Christian Belief*, 78–9.

[157] This 'pure' nature may have less to do with Aquinas than with some of his later interpreters, and it is arguable that Henri de Lubac's *nouvelle théologie* reaction against it is more faithful to Aquinas' thinking than are the understandings of those interpreters. Newton himself, we might note, had a more complex view than some of his successors, based in part on much earlier arguments about the divine will – see Oakley, 'Christian Theology and the Newtonian Science'.

gaps in current scientific explanation, and God became, for many, what has been called 'the God of the gaps'.

This had an effect on the initial response of Christians to Charles Darwin's understanding of evolution, since many of them objected to that understanding less because they defended a literalist interpretation of the Genesis creation accounts than because Darwinism challenged their picture of the process of creation as a series of supernatural acts. But, as Aubrey Moore pointed out at the time, their picture of 'special creation' was theologically questionable because its notion of occasional divine intervention implied 'as its correlative a theory of ordinary absence'.[158] This ordinary absence was, however, intrinsic to the 'God of the gaps' outlook that many Western Christians by this time espoused, and it is precisely against this understanding that many participants in the science-theology dialogue have reacted by insisting, with Moore, that God's immanence in the cosmos must be stressed in any valid account of divine action.

This reaction came to a head in an influential series of conferences and publications between 1988 and 2003. This was arranged jointly by the Vatican Observatory and the Center for Theology and the Natural Sciences in Berkeley. The dominant view that arose from this 'Divine Action Project' was one that assumed it to be necessary for God to supplement what Western theological systems usually call the 'general divine action' that arises straightforwardly from the regularities of the natural world. In this view, it is necessary also to defend the concept of 'special divine action', which is regarded as coming into effect when God 'responds' to events in the world – to intercessory prayer, for example – through some mechanism which, while it may make use of natural processes, is not analysable solely in terms of those processes.[159] At a conceptual level, this approach came to rely on the way in which physics – through the development of quantum mechanics in the early twentieth century – had moved away from the deterministic, clockwork model of the universe implied by the Newtonian understanding and towards a probabilistic understanding.

For many Western theologians, one of the attractive features of this scientific abandonment of determinism was that it seems to allow for 'special' divine action that does not require the kind of divine intervention in which the laws of nature are set aside in order that God may act directly. The simplest and earliest model of how this could occur – that popularized by William Pollard – was, in fact, based straightforwardly on quantum mechanical insights, in that he saw quantum indeterminacy as leaving room for God to affect the outcome of

---

[158] Moore, *Science and Faith*, 73.
[159] A summary of this project is given in Wildman, 'The Divine Action Project, 1988 to 2003'.

particular quantum events.[160] Since Pollard's advocacy of this model, however, its problematic aspects have been pointed out by John Polkinghorne, although it is still seen as valid by some.[161] Still, the concept of some comparable sort of temporal 'causal joint' between God and the world remains a central aspect of the Western – and especially Protestant – exploration of the interface of science and theology. (In the Roman Catholic world, the influence of an alternative scholastic scheme of 'primary' and 'secondary' causes is often pursued. However, this has yet to become a dominant strategy within the dialogue, not least because it has been widely attacked by influential participants in the dialogue, such as John Polkinghorne.)[162]

If the world is not deterministic but simply probabilistic, it is held, then there might in principle be a number of ways in which God could affect events in the world without setting aside the laws of nature. For Polkinghorne, for example, quantum mechanical and chaotic phenomena seem to point to the reality of a more 'subtle and supple' universe than those phenomena in themselves indicate – one in which the 'cloudy unpredictabilities of physical process' can be interpreted as 'the sites of ontological openness'.[163] For Peacocke, God is seen as acting on the 'world as a whole' in such a way that specific, local providential events are brought about through a process of 'whole-part constraint'. This scheme takes its bearings from the way in which complex wholes can, in scientific perspective, be seen as having an effect on the parts of which they are made up.[164]

There are a number of objections to all of these schemes, however.[165] One of these relates to the way in which they are often described as 'noninterventionist' when in practice they have not abandoned temporal divine interference with the world at all but only a particular kind of 'supernatural intervention'. The fact that interference is still envisaged is absolutely clear, since those who advocate

---

[160] Pollard, *Chance and Providence*.

[161] Polkinghorne, *Faith, Science and Understanding*, 120–1, comments that there are three main difficulties: (1) quantum uncertainties 'tend to cancel each other out' at scales other than the extremely small; (2) only measurements are relevant and these are only occasional 'so that agency exercised in this way would have a curiously sporadic character'; (3) macroscopic consequences can only arise from microscopic quantum events if – as in certain situations in which chaos theory becomes relevant – there is 'an enhancement of their effect due to their being part of a much larger system which is extremely sensitive to the fine details of circumstances'.

[162] See, for example, Polkinghorne, *Faith, Science and Understanding*, 115–17. For a brief but more sympathetic study of this 'primary and secondary causes' approach in the context of the science-theology dialogue, see Silva, 'Divine Action and Thomism'.

[163] Polkinghorne, *Scientists As Theologians*, 40.

[164] Peacocke, 'God's Interaction with the World', 283.

[165] For some of these objections, which will not be discussed further here, see Knight, *The God of Nature*, 22–7.

this kind of causal joint scheme still have an implicit picture in which two outcomes of any situation are possible. One is that which nature, *left to itself* (in the sense of simply being sustained in being by God), would probably bring about. The other is that which will come about if God chooses to respond to events in the world in a *direct, temporal* way, through some kind of manipulation that is not incompatible with the laws of nature that He has ordained. (Here, we should note, while formal notions of supernatural intervention may have been abandoned, these formal notions seem often to have left as their legacy a kind of quasi-instinctive sense that God must act from 'outside' of the created order.)[166]

This picture of two essentially separate modes of divine action – sustaining the natural order and manipulating it – is, we should note, based at least in part upon a picture of God that is, from an Orthodox perspective, questionable in two ways. First, it involves a notion of God as a *temporal* being. God is seen, in events of 'special' divine action, as *responding* to events in the world much as any other temporal agent must. The notion of God's eternal and timeless being – central to both Eastern and Western theologies before the modern period – is effectively ignored. (It is notable, in this respect, that this temporal scheme seems to have had less influence among Roman Catholic participants in the science-theology dialogue than among Protestants, since these Catholics tend to accept Aquinas' notion of God's eternity and, as we have noted, to look at divine action in terms of the scholastic distinction between primary and secondary causes. Quite rightly, Wesley Wildman has observed that the causal joint approach represents 'a distinctively Protestant deviation from the mainstream classical view'.)[167]

The second – and often related – oversimplification in this causal joint scheme is to regard God as one who acts in a way that is comparable to the way in which a created agent does: as a 'person'.[168] There is little or no sense that speaking about God as personal should be understood in an apophatic way,[169] nor is there any sense of God as a Trinity of persons, whose action is 'from the Father, through the Son, and in (or by) the Holy Spirit'. (As we shall see in Section 7, the Christological approach that I shall advocate in this section, on the basis of the Orthodox doctrine of creation, arguably complements

---

[166] Here, once again, understandings developed within the *nouvelle théologie* movement might have played an important role in combatting this instinctive approach, but in general this has not been the case among participants in the dialogue.

[167] Wildman, 'Robert John Russell's Theology of God's Action', 166.

[168] A significant factor in the divine action project was the kind of understanding exemplified by the comment that 'to deny the temporality of God is to deny that he is personal in any sense in which we understand personality' (Lucas, 'The Temporality of God', 236).

[169] See Knight, 'An Apophatic Approach to God's "Personal" Nature'.

a minority Protestant understanding that focuses on the Holy Spirit, thereby pointing to a fully Trinitarian understanding of divine action.)

But it is not only in terms such as these that the causal joint scheme for understanding divine action is questionable. Even when looked at in terms of its own conceptual framework, this model proves to be so problematic that – as Nicholas Saunders has said in his examination of the topic – contemporary Western theology '*is in a crisis*'.[170] As we shall see in Section 6, however, the kind of *impasse* in which, according to Saunders, the supporters of the causal joint scheme find themselves has its origin in their inadequate conceptual scheme. For, if contemporary Western theology is indeed in a crisis in its exploration of divine action, this crisis is not just due to the difficulty of finding a coherent causal joint model for 'special' acts of God. The problem lies also in the inadequacy of the prevalent understanding of the essentially autonomous character of the natural world, which leads – even among Western proponents of various kinds of panentheism[171] – to the belief that acts of this kind are necessary.

The very different form of panentheism that is intrinsic to the Orthodox understanding of creation points, however, towards a different conceptual framework for considering divine action, based on the teleological aspect of Maximus' understanding. Few outside of the Eastern Orthodox community are, admittedly, likely to accept the details of Maximus' philosophical articulation of this framework, but its relevance to them does not depend on such acceptance. It depends, rather, on his 'theological instinct' that the world – *as part of the very nature given to it by God in His act of creation* – has what we might call a *teleological-Christological* character. This instinct points, I have suggested, towards the way in which all divine action may be seen in terms of a kind of *strong theistic naturalism* – a term which may be defined simply as any theistic understanding in which the validity of the concept of temporal 'special divine action' is denied.[172]

---

[170] Saunders, *Divine Action and Modern Science*, 215 (emphasis in original).

[171] Some Western scholars have tried to address some of the problems of the causal joint approach by adopting a *panentheistic* framework of the somewhat vague form that we have noted in Section 4. However, the fact that these Western forms of panentheism do not really solve the problems of the causal joint model is indicated by the fact that Western scholars who reject panentheism and those who identify themselves as panentheists do not differ in any significant way in relation to the model's conceptual basis. The understanding of the anti-panentheist John Polkinghorne, for example, is essentially no different from that of panentheists such as Philip Clayton and Arthur Peacocke. While advocating panentheism, these latter scholars still pose questions about divine action in a way that relies, at least implicitly, on an older model in which a separation between God and the world is assumed. (See Knight, 'Panentheism and the Word Made Flesh'.)

[172] The qualifying word *strong* is necessary in order to distinguish the approach that is being considered here from that involved in Arthur Peacocke's description of himself as a theistic

The best-known historical manifestation of *strong theistic naturalism* is, of course, the deism of the eighteenth century, and this has been a problem because many have seen such a naturalism as intrinsically deistic. However, not only was the concept of 'special divine action' eschewed by the deists but what was seen as possible through 'general divine action' was extremely limited. They could not, for example, see intercessory prayer as having any purpose (other, perhaps, than that of refining the religious sensibilities of those who indulge in it). The possibility that there can be some sort of 'response' to such prayer was simply precluded by their understanding. It is important to recognize, therefore, that this view is not, philosophically, the only option available to the strong theistic naturalist. A naturalistic view, in itself, simply assumes that the cosmos develops in a consistent way according to divinely given 'fixed instructions' of a law-like kind. The possibility that such instructions can bring about subtle and appropriate 'responses' to events in the world is not one that can be precluded in principle.

This is something that may be seen, as I have indicated elsewhere, through the analogy of human providential action.[173] The example I have given is that of the situation in which young adults are away from home but still financially dependent on their parents, such as when they are studying at a university. In this situation, parents can arrange their financial support through setting up standing orders to a bank. Such orders not only can include instructions about the transfer of money on a regular basis for general living expenses – the equivalent of 'general' action as usually understood – but can also anticipate specific needs that may or may not occur. Such an order can, for example, include an instruction to pay for the cost of repairs to the student's car if they become necessary. An instruction of this sort has the effect of 'special' provi- dence – in that it brings about action in response to a specific rather than a general need – even though it comes about through a 'secondary cause' mechanism of the 'general action' kind, and no new action on the part of the prime agent is necessary.

This analogy is not, we should note, intended to elucidate the mechanism of divine action, though some have used it as such.[174] It is intended simply to illustrate an important principle: that strong theistic naturalism can be con- structed in such a way that the scope of general divine action is not limited in the

---

naturalist. His advocacy of a distinction between 'special' and 'general' modes of divine action means that he is a proponent only of a 'weak' theistic naturalism, not of a 'strong' model of the kind discussed here, in which that distinction between these modes is made redundant.

[173] The argument that follows was first set out (with slightly different wording) in Knight, *The God of Nature*, 28–9.

[174] See, for example, Darg, 'Cosmic If-Statements'.

way that the deists assumed. 'Responses' of a providential sort can be the result of a 'fixed instruction' mechanism that is – while 'impersonal' in mechanism – far from impersonal in either the giver's intention or the recipient's perception.

Once this principle is accepted, we are enabled, without unnecessary constraints, to consider a 'naturalistic' teleological-Christological model of divine action based on Maximus' insights, in which all things are drawn – by their very nature and not by some external 'force' – not only towards the eschatological state but also towards various intermediate goals associated with the journey towards that state. Not the least of these intermediate goals is the emergence of human beings through the kind of convergent evolution on which Conway Morris has focused. In principle, however, anything that contributes towards the journey to the eschatological state – including 'responses' to intercessory prayer – would seem to be possible in terms of this 'naturalistic' model.

Moreover, this view of divine providence can even incorporate the Christ event through what might be seen as an Orthodox version of 'evolutionary Christology'. One Orthodox scholar, Paul Ladouceur, has analysed a number of patristic notions that point towards an understanding in which the goal of evolution is not simply humans 'but rather the Incarnation of the Logos'.[175] Another, Mark Chenoweth, focuses on Maximus the Confessor's understanding and argues that 'seen through a Maximian framework, the end of evolution is not merely the advent of human beings, but a particular human being: Christ'.[176]

Whatever we may make of this kind of evolutionary Christology – with its roots in a far more traditional theological understanding than is usually the case with such Christologies[177] – the important thing to note here is that the general teleological-Christological model of divine action that I have outlined would seem to have several advantages in the context of the current debate about divine action within the science-theology dialogue. By allowing us to transcend the need for any distinction to be made between what 'nature' can 'do on its own' (i.e. when simply sustained in being by God) and what can only be done through some 'special' mode of divine action, a neo-Byzantine model of this sort would allow us to see God's presence and action in the cosmos simply as two sides of the same coin. In this respect, it simply denies the distinction between 'general' and 'special' modes of divine action, as usually understood,

---

[175] Ladouceur, 'Evolution and Genesis 2–3', 162.

[176] Chenoweth, 'A Maximian Framework for Understanding Evolution', 175.

[177] Conservative Western Christians often react to any 'evolutionary Christology' with horror because of the tendency of Western forms of such Christology to rely on a 'liberal' understanding of Christ as no more than a Spirit-filled human being. In the Orthodox version, however, there is no such tendency.

and tends towards the sort of Thomistic model that speaks in terms of primary and secondary causes, providing that model with a far more definitive theological grounding than it has usually been given.

Yet, we may ask, even if the incarnation fits into this picture, in the way suggested by Ladouceur and Chenoweth, how do other events of the kind usually thought of as 'miraculous' fit into it? The model that speaks in terms of primary and secondary causes has usually viewed such events as ones in which there is no natural, 'secondary' cause, so that supernatural intervention is the only explanation. Must this be the case also if we accept a teleological-Christological model of divine action? As we shall see in Section 6, there are both philosophical considerations and resources within the Orthodox tradition that suggest otherwise.

6 Naturalism and the 'Miraculous'

The laws of nature that can be provisionally identified are those that can be explored through the scientific methodology, which relies on the repeatability of observation or experiment and on the discernibility of cause and effect. We need to recognize, however, that it may be simplistic to preclude the possibility of an 'enhanced' naturalism in which it is acknowledged that the cosmos may obey not only the laws that can be identified in this way but also other 'fixed instructions' that are not straightforwardly susceptible to this investigative methodology.

Indeed, this is something that may even seem likely when we consider the effects of complexity and emergence. Not only are practical repeatability and discernible cause and effect characteristic of only relatively simple systems, which can be effectively isolated from factors that would obscure these characteristics, but, in addition, important issues related to reductionism in the sciences suggest the necessity of positing laws or organizing principles of a kind that are not susceptible to ordinary scientific investigation but can only be inferred from their general effect.[178]

This focus on complexity has important ramifications for our response to anecdotal evidence of phenomena of the kind sometimes labelled *paranormal*. It suggests that it is simplistic to see such phenomena as spurious because of their lack of susceptibility to investigation through normal laboratory methods. The failure of these methods may simply indicate that such phenomena occur only in situations of considerable complexity or extremity. Once this is recognized, the supposed impossibility of paranormal phenomena becomes

---

[178] The current state of debate about emergence is well represented in the essays in Clayton and Davies, *The Re-emergence of Emergence*.

questionable, and the question of the weight that we should give to the anecdotal evidence for such phenomena becomes an important one.

In attempting to understand the religiously significant events that we regard as miraculous, it may be prudent – at least initially – to use this term *paranormal* rather than the term *miraculous*. This is because the latter term is frequently understood by Western Christians in terms of their quasi-instinctive understanding of what the term *supernatural* means, which is arguably far removed not only from Orthodox usage but even from classic Western understandings.[179] What Orthodoxy (and those classic Western understandings) stress is not so much the distinction between the natural and the supernatural as that between the *created* and the *uncreated*. (This distinction is highlighted in Orthodoxy by the way in which, as Elizabeth Theokritoff has remarked, Orthodox thinking envisages the created order as 'a structure in which vastly incommensurate elements – angelic, human, animate and inanimate – are all held together and function as a coherent whole, focused on their Creator').[180]

Over and above this consideration, the term *supernatural* – with its implication, when applied to 'miraculous' events, that the laws of nature have been set aside in favour of some direct action of God – may, as we shall see, be a misleading translation of the Eastern patristic notion of events that are *above nature*. The implications of the term *supernatural*, as they are often understood in the West, need not, therefore, be seen by Orthodox Christians as an intrinsic part of their understanding of the 'miraculous' events that they certainly believe have occurred. A flexibility of thought becomes possible in which an explanation of such events in terms of an 'enhanced' naturalism becomes conceivable, since – as we have already noted – the Orthodox tradition 'knows nothing of "pure nature" to which grace is added as a supernatural gift'.[181]

If we ask why it is that most scientists do not accept that paranormal events occur, a major factor is their methodological stress on the importance of *repeatability*. To be accepted as scientific evidence, what is observed by one researcher in one laboratory or observatory must be observable by another researcher in another laboratory or observatory. Reported phenomena that are

---

[179] Aquinas, for example, uses the term 'supernatural' (and related terms) only rarely – 336 times in more than 8.5 million words – and he never does so in the way which is now common (even within the Roman Catholic Church) in which, for example, angels are often spoken of as 'supernatural beings' rather than as what the traditional usage of both East and West would demand: as non-corporeal beings within the created order. Popular usage is, however, now such that 'angels, demons, and discarnate human spirits . . . are usually classed as supernatural' and this represents 'the everyday usage among people of ordinary intelligence and generally among their superiors' (Knight, 'The Definition of the Supernatural', 360.)

[180] Theokritoff, 'Creator and Creation', 65–6.

[181] Lossky, *The Mystical Theology of the Eastern Church*, 101.

not susceptible to this repeatability criterion are rightly ignored as *scientific* evidence. The question remains, however, of whether rational agents should entirely ignore anecdotal evidence of paranormal events simply because this repeatability criterion is apparently violated. Many scientists, in the face of violation of this criterion, now simply dismiss the possibility of such phenomena, putting all anecdotal evidence of their occurrence down to fraud, wishful thinking, or pure coincidence. Others, however, consider that the strength of at least some of this anecdotal evidence is such as to suggest that phenomena of this sort do occur.

If we take the view that paranormal events do occur – as most Christians do in relation to the events they tend to label 'miraculous' – how are we to understand these events? Should we think of them as examples of the laws of nature being violated? Much depends on how we understand the concept of laws of nature. Some, for example, will assume that the laws of nature are always in principle susceptible to scientific investigation. Other than in terms of violation of those laws, therefore, they will be unable to conceptualize events that are reported but seem not to be susceptible to this mode of investigation. Others may assume that laws of nature will always correspond to a 'common sense' understanding of the kinds of thing that are possible. These will, once again, conceptualize paranormal events as necessarily being violations of these laws. However, the effects of holistic factors and of emergent complexity may make the first of these assumptions invalid, while physicists in particular will realize that reliance on a 'common sense' criterion is very questionable. (This is perhaps the reason that they less often seem to be strident atheists than biologists are.) Not only do relativity and quantum mechanics notoriously defy 'common sense' but physicists are also aware of historical examples of unpredicted phenomena that at the time of their first observation seemed impossible in terms of current understanding.

The simplest example of this is perhaps the phenomenon of the complete disappearance of electrical resistance in certain materials when they are cooled to below a certain threshold temperature. Discovered as a phenomenon in 1911, this *superconductivity* was soon accepted as a genuine aspect of the natural world because of its repeatability, but it resisted adequate theoretical explanation for several decades. This phenomenon provides an example of what scientists sometimes call *regime change*, in which there is a discontinuity in physical properties when certain conditions are met – in this case, the properties of certain materials and very low temperature. It is not that the laws of nature have changed or been violated but rather that, in certain circumstances, potential effects which are 'normally' inoperative become significant in their effects.

It has sometimes been suggested by Western Christian commentators that regime change of this kind provides a possible analogy for our thinking about miracles.[182] (Indeed, Robert John Russell has even suggested that Christ's resurrection may be seen in comparable terms, as 'the first instantiation of a new law of nature'.)[183] Is this, we must ask, a possible way forward for us in thinking about 'miraculous' events in general, and even about the resurrection itself? Such a way of speaking seems, at first sight, to undermine the role of God in such happenings, but three things should prevent us from assuming that this must necessarily be the case.

One of these is that not only Orthodox Christianity but also medieval scholasticism and the modern Western theology of nature stress that God is present and active in all natural processes. What happens through those processes is, therefore, not (as in a deistic understanding) something with which God is not directly involved. Second, there is a sense in which, for any Christian understanding, all God's actions are susceptible in principle to the kind of understanding that lies behind our thinking about laws of nature. Christians assume God's *consistency*, so that if certain circumstances are found, then certain consequences may be expected to follow. The third thing that we need to consider is, however, perhaps the most important from an Orthodox perspective. This is that something similar to this regime change analogy was occasionally hinted at in the patristic era.

In particular, in the work of Augustine of Hippo – here not in conflict with Eastern patristic perspectives in the way that he sometimes was – there is a clear implication that highly unusual events are able to occur because, over and above the natural laws that we are able to understand, there is a 'higher' law-like framework that the cosmos also obeys, which is in practice beyond human understanding. If there are simple systems that are susceptible to our understanding in terms of the 'lower' law, this is only, Augustine seems to suggest, because the threshold has not been reached at which the influences of this 'higher' component of the way the cosmos operates become operative.[184]

There are a number of philosophical and theological aspects of this view.[185] One, which is of particular importance, relates to the way in which, although patristic use of the notion of events being 'above nature' is not entirely uniform, it may often be seen as having more in common with the modern notion of *paranormal* events than it does with the notion of *supernatural* events as these

---

[182] See, for example, Polkinghorne, *One World*, 74-6
[183] Russell, 'Bodily Resurrection, Eschatology, and Scientific Cosmology', 3.
[184] Pannenberg, 'The Concept of Miracle'.
[185] See Knight, *Science and the Christian Faith*, 197–207, in which the considerations set out here are supplemented by further philosophical and theological considerations.

are usually (if not universally) now understood in the West.[186] For when something occurs that is expressed by the patristic writers as being 'above nature', the term *nature* is usually being used by them to describe nature as we commonly experience it. However, some of them also speak, in a different context, about something rather different: the *true* nature of the cosmos as it was originally created and envisaged by God, which is to be re-established in an enhanced form when that cosmos attains its eschatological state. It is – as we shall see in Section 7 – the relationship between these two 'natures' that is arguably at the heart of the Eastern patristic understanding of 'miraculous' events.

7 An Eschatologically Focused and Trinitarian Understanding

From an Orthodox point of view, while mainstream Western theology has tended to overstress the effects of the Fall on human noetic perception, it has rarely, if ever, properly acknowledged the radical difference between the 'external' aspects of the empirical world and the world as it is in God's ultimate intention for it. Orthodox Christians tend to express this ultimate intention not only by looking forward to the eschatological state but also by 'looking backwards' to the Paradise from which, according to the Genesis story, our first ancestors were expelled. This story, according to Orthodox understanding, indicates that God's 'original' world has had to be radically modified by Him because of the rebellion of His creatures. Indeed, in a theological sense – though not in the philosophical sense in which the term 'natural' is usually used – we should see the empirical world in which we live as 'unnatural' or – perhaps better – 'subnatural'.

This perception allows Orthodox to move beyond Western theology's tendency to see the biblical concept of the Fall as having implications only for humanity rather than for the entire cosmos and provides an important resource for the resolution of two major problems faced by theologians in the West: that which is usually called the problem of natural evil and that of how God may be said to act to bring about 'miraculous' events.

Western philosophical approaches to the problem of evil may be correct when they suggest that human life and choice are only possible against a background of regularity which necessarily has unwanted effects. They may also be correct – as Irenaeus' thought suggests – that evil is a necessary aspect of a world which is

---

[186] Once again, the *nouvelle théologie* movement provides an interesting modification to earlier Western understandings, especially in relation to its rediscovery of a sacramental understanding comparable to the Orthodox one. See Boersma, 'Nature and the Supernatural in *la nouvelle théologie*'.

a 'vale of soul-making'.[187] In their different ways, however, such approaches assume that our understanding of the link between this world and the 'new creation' can be developed only in terms of the way in which the problematic aspects of the former may be assumed to be necessary to provide conditions through which the latter may be attained. God's will can in some sense, it is assumed, encompass the evil in the world because a greater good is derived from that evil. While this is little more than a faith-based assertion for Western theological approaches, however, the Orthodox tradition has a resource here that Western traditions have, at best, only in a diluted form. This is the understanding of the 'garments of skin' (Genesis 3:21) that we have already looked at briefly in Section 3.

In modern Orthodox writing, this notion has been examined in considerable detail in Panayiotis Nellas's book *Deification in Christ*. Even before the Fall, says Nellas – reflecting a view found in Irenaeus and others – man had 'need of salvation, since he was an imperfect and incomplete "child"'.[188] Christ accomplishes man's salvation 'not only in a negative way, liberating him from the consequences of original sin, but also in a positive way, completing his iconic, prelapsarian "being"'.[189]

The notion of the empirical world as less than fully natural is, says Nellas, central to 'the teaching of the Fathers on human nature', which 'forms, as it were, a bridge with two piers'. The first pier, he goes on, is 'the understanding of what is "in the image"'. The second is 'the deeply significant notion of "garments of skin"'. These garments of skin are to be interpreted partly in terms of what is necessary for survival in man's postlapsarian state but also partly in terms of the need to foster in a more positive way 'his return to what is "in the image"'.[190]

Intrinsic to the notion of the garments of skin is, says Nellas, the notion of mortality. The Fall, he says, though in one sense a fall into materiality, is not to be identified simply with a fall into created matter. According to Gregory of Nyssa, for example, although the body has become 'coarse and solid' through the Fall and is characterized by a 'gross and heavy composition', it will, at the general resurrection, recover its prelapsarian state, being 'respun' into 'something lighter and more aerial'. The body will not be left behind, as a Gnostic dualism might maintain, but will be transfigured into its 'original' beauty. Moreover, as we have seen in Section 3, it is not only the body that is, for Gregory, in need of this transformation. He insists that the functions of the soul must also undergo a transformation, having become 'corporeal' through the

---

[187] An interesting analysis of this 'vale of soul making' idea is to be found in Hick, *Evil and the God of Love*.
[188] Nellas, *Deification in Christ*, 37.   [189] Ibid., 39.   [190] Ibid., 44.

Fall.[191] Thus, while Gregory, more than most patristic writers, may seem to identify the garments of skin with the postlapsarian human body, he is, according to Nellas, actually 'referring to the entire postlapsarian psychosomatic clothing of the human person'.[192]

An important point here, says Nellas, is that, although at one level the garments of skin are an evil, brought about as a direct result of human rebellion against the divine intention, God 'changes that which is the result of denial and is therefore negative into something relatively positive'. The garments of skin are therefore, he goes on, 'a second blessing to a self-exiled humanity'. God has added this blessing 'like a second nature to the existing human nature, so that by using it correctly humanity can survive and realize its original goal in Christ'.[193] Moreover, says Nellas, it is not only such obvious evils as death that can be seen in this way. Following John Chrysostom, he relates the garments of skin to human work, to the arts and sciences, and to politics. In these aspects of human life, he says, we can see particularly clearly how the garments of skin 'are not unrelated to the iconic faculties of man before the fall'. God, he goes on, has enabled 'the attributes of that which is "in the image" – the attributes which were transformed into "garments of skin" without being changed in essence – to be useful to man not only in his struggle for mere survival but also as a means of making the new journey towards God'.[194]

An aspect of the garments of skin that Nellas also discusses is their relationship to the more general cosmic ramifications of the Fall. The laws which govern that order, while they continue to operate after the Fall, are seen as doing so in a way which allows what the West calls 'natural' evil – that is, they operate 'in a disorganized and disordered way, and they involve man too in this disordered operation with the result that they draw him into misery and anguish'.[195] These cosmic implications of the Fall have, however, also been transformed by God. Like the human garments of skin, they constitute not only a penalty but also a remedy.[196]

For those who seek to be sensitive to modern science, an important question arises at this point: that of whether this vision – of a cosmos with a 'fallen' character that in some sense has its origins in human rebellion against God – can still be accepted. At one level, it clearly has its attractions since, as we have seen, it can supplement in a subtle and powerful way the kind of perspective on the problem of natural evil that has been developed by Western Christians in a more purely philosophical manner. At another level, however, a major question arises: that of whether we can give any significant weight to an

---

[191] Ibid., 50–1.   [192] Ibid., 50.   [193] Ibid., 61.   [194] Ibid., 90–1.   [195] Ibid., 62.
[196] Ibid., 63 (note 128).

understanding that is apparently tied so inextricably to a notion of the Fall as a *historical* event. This notion of a Fall within cosmic history is clearly incompatible with our scientific understanding of the world because it is evident, if we accept that understanding, that evil did not enter the world only after some historical event in which humans rebelled against God. Death, for example, clearly existed long before the evolutionary emergence of humans, as did painful diseases of the kind that are sometimes evident in the fossil remains of dinosaurs.

Before we conclude that the traditional understanding of the Fall must be abandoned, however, we must ask precisely what it was that was at the heart of that understanding. Here, it is important to recognize that Orthodox thinking about this issue has not always seen the 'sequence' set out in Genesis – of creation, Fall, and 'this world' – in simple historical terms. Interesting questions about the traditional understanding of the Fall and its cosmic effects have, for example, been posed in recent years by Orthodox scholars such as Christos Yannaras and Paul Ladouceur, while even in the patristic era similar questions seem to have arisen from the effects of Origen's speculations.[197]

One example of this aspect of patristic thinking is related to the way in which, as we have seen, some in that era believed, with Gregory of Nyssa, that our present body has become coarse and solid through the Fall but will, at the general resurrection, recover its 'prelapsarian' state. This was understood, according to Nellas, in terms of the way in which our existence in the paradisal state should not be identified with our current biological make-up, which is an aspect of the 'garments of skin' given to us by God. Rather, as he puts it, God, by 'allowing man to dress himself in biological life, the fruit of sin . . . redirected death, which was also the fruit of sin, against biological life, and thus by death is put to death not man but the corruption which clothes him'.[198] In a related way, the Fall was often seen, in the patristic era, as being a transition not only into our present biological state but also into time as we now experience it. As Philip Sherrard has put it, it was a lapse '*into* a materialized space-time universe'.[199] In this perspective, the expulsion from Paradise involved much more of a discontinuity than is often appreciated, since not only was our 'original' life not biological life but it was, in addition, not even a temporal existence in the usual sense of that term.

This kind of understanding of the character of our unfallen state has been explored by modern Orthodox scholars like Sergius Bulgakov, who have suggested that the Fall should be seen not as a historical event but as a 'meta-historical'

[197] See Yannaras, *The Enigma of Evil*; Ladouceur, 'Evolution and Genesis 2–3'.
[198] Nellas, *Deification in Christ*, 64.   [199] Sherrard, *Christianity and Eros*, 26 (my emphasis).

one.[200] This may be a somewhat difficult concept to understand, but just as Nellas himself speaks in another context of 'the supra-temporal reality of God',[201] so also it may be necessary to talk about the 'pre'-lapsarian state of humanity in comparable supratemporal terms.

This idea is reinforced, moreover, when we recognize that, in the thinking of Maximus the Confessor, the Fall is seen as so inevitable in created things that creation and Fall are seen as simultaneous, so that for him – as one modern scholar has put it – 'any actual, prelapsarian existence is purely hypothetical'.[202] In this kind of understanding, which is reflected in the thinking of some modern Orthodox scholars, createdness and fallenness are so strongly connected that the Fall narrative points not to a lost historical state but to a kind of 'nostalgia' for paradise that is part of our psychological make-up, an intrinsic aspect of which is an urge towards our eschatological 'return' to Paradise. (The Orthodox funeral service speaks of returning to 'the longed-for homeland', while the near-universality of some kind of lost Paradise myth points to this longing as an intrinsic aspect of human religiosity.)

If this perspective is valid, then, while it may be too much of a generalization to say – as Robin Amis does – that, when early Christian thinkers write of the Fall, they write of it 'not as a historical event' but as a 'psychological event', this comment does point us towards an important component of patristic thought.[203] What the fall narrative indicates, in this framework, is not a 'historical' scenario that is in conflict with modern scientific perspectives. Rather, it ties God's 'original' creation of a 'good' cosmos more firmly to the eschatological state than to the empirical world of our present experience, so that the paradisal state to which we 'look back' – whether psychologically or in scriptural texts – is not a genuine historical memory but a pointer towards God's ultimate intentions.[204] We are enabled, through the 'memory' of Paradise, to see more clearly that the situation of frustration, meaninglessness, and evil in which we find ourselves in 'this world' is not part of God's ultimate intention for us.

In terms of this kind of understanding, our present empirical situation, however we think it came about, is not a *natural* one at all, if we use that term to refer to God's original and ultimate intentions (as Orthodox writers tend to do). The notions of the 'subnatural' state of our present universe and of the garments of skin are, therefore, not ones that are irrelevant to us, even if we have

---

[200] Bulgakov, *Bride of the Lamb*, 164-6   [201] Nellas, *Deification in Christ*, 35.

[202] Cooper, *The Body in St. Maximus the Confessor*, 80.

[203] Amis, *A Different Christianity*, 48.

[204] Here, John Haught's notion of the ontological priority of the future provides a slightly different (but arguably complementary) way of expressing the same insight. See Haught, *God after Darwin*.

reservations about the particular way in which they were originally formulated or are sometimes now understood. Whatever our reservations may be, these notions still provide a subtle and illuminating perspective on God's intentions – intentions which are, according to Christian belief, to be fully consummated in the 'world to come'. Ours is not the truly natural world that God saw as 'good' at the time of its creation but a distorted version of that world, albeit with grace still perceptible in its modes of operation.

This understanding is highly relevant to the question of how we may speak of God acting 'miraculously' in a world characterized by obedience to 'laws of nature'. For the Orthodox tradition – while sometimes speaking about God acting in a way that is 'above' nature – has tended, as we have noted, to avoid the kind of distinction between the natural and the supernatural often used in the West. Rather, because of the Orthodox view that there is 'no natural or normal state, since grace is implied in the act of creation itself',[205] Orthodox theologians have tended to think about divine action and the miraculous in a far more subtle (if usually less systematic) way than has been characteristic of Western writers.

This may be illustrated by the question of how God acts in and through the sacraments (or, as Orthodox tend to call them, the 'mysteries') of the church. For Orthodox scholars – as, in a less focused way, for the Western scholar, Arthur Peacocke[206] – a sacrament is not only what it is for most Western Christians: an outward and visible sign of an inward and spiritual grace. It is also something more: what Alexander Schmemann calls 'a revelation of the genuine *nature* of creation'.[207] Philip Sherrard, in particular, has stressed this aspect of the Eastern patristic understanding, noting that a sacrament is not 'something set over against, or existing outside, the rest of life ... something extrinsic, and fixed in its extrinsicality, as if by some sort of magical operation or *Deus ex machina* the sacramental object is suddenly turned into something other than itself'. On the contrary, he goes on, 'what is indicated or revealed in the sacrament is something universal, the intrinsic sanctity and spirituality of all things, what one might call their real nature'.[208]

What makes the sacrament necessary, Sherrard goes on to explain, is simply the way in which the Fall has led to the created order's 'estrangement and alienation from its intrinsic nature'. In the sacrament, he says, 'this divided, estranged and alienated state is transcended' and the created order's 'essential and intrinsic nature is revealed'.[209] This means, he continues, that the sacrament

---

[205] Lossky, *The Mystical Theology of the Eastern Church*, 101.

[206] See Knight, *Wrestling with the Divine*, 17–22, for a discussion of what I have called the 'pansacramentalism' of Peacocke's outlook.

[207] Schmemann, *The Eucharist*, 33–4.   [208] Sherrard, 'The Sacrament', 134.   [209] Ibid., 135.

is 'reality itself, as it is in its naked essence and without anything being changed or symbolized or substituted'. Because of this, he says, terms such as 'transubstantiation' or 'transformation' are ones which 'tend to lead to confusion', since at the deepest level 'nothing need be transubstantiated or transformed'. The sacrament is a transformation only insofar as it is 'a re-creation of the world "as it was in the beginning"'.[210] In this understanding, there is no limit to the number of sacraments because a sacrament is simply a manifestation of the true reality of some aspect of this world, in which its usual relative opaqueness to God's purposes for it, and presence within it, gives way to a complete transparency.

This notion of the potential for any part of the created order to become more fully transparent to the purposes and presence of God is an extremely important one when we come to consider God's action in more general terms. For while the created order evidently has a certain transparency to the purposes of God before any specific human invocation of divine grace, it is clearly not fully transparent to those purposes prior to that invocation. The way in which the universe has evolved naturalistically does, certainly, already indicate some degree of transparency to the divine purpose, as does the fact that its beauty can lead us directly to praise God as its creator. But as the problem of natural evil indicates, this transparency is only relative. In a 'fallen' world there is also a degree of opaqueness to God's purposes. However – as the centrality of intercessory prayer to the Christian tradition indicates – this opaqueness may be overcome, and what Western Christians call God's 'special' providence can be brought about, through the human recognition and invocation of God's will.

From this perspective, divine action may be illuminated by the nature of the sacramental mysteries in a profound way. Quite simply, the 'miraculous' events that Western theologians have usually spoken of in terms of God's 'special' action may be seen not as the product of some kind of divine interference with the world, in which the laws of nature are set aside or manipulated. Rather, they may be seen as the outward manifestation in this world of something that is already present but hidden within it – what we can properly call its 'natural' state. The miraculous is not, in this perspective, the result of something being added to the world. It is, rather, the wiping away from that world of the grime of its fallen state, in order to reveal it in its pristine splendour.

In this perspective, while the old Western distinction between 'general' and 'special' modes of divine action is rendered superfluous, at another level the distinction can remain meaningful. Its new meaning lies, however, not in the traditional Western distinction between modes of divine action but in

---

[210] Ibid., 139.

a distinction between different degrees of human response to the divine will. 'General' divine action corresponds to those aspects of the world that are, independently of the human response to God, still sufficiently transparent for God's purposes to be fulfilled. These will include all those naturalistic and scientifically explorable processes which have allowed the evolutionary emergence of beings who can respond to God in faith. 'Special' divine action may be seen as corresponding to those 'natural' aspects of the world which are, so to speak, present but inoperative until that response is made.

When the universe 'changes' so as to bring about events of 'special' providence, it is a sign and a foretaste of what is 'naturally' to be when all the purposes of God have been fulfilled. In such an event, created things are, in the deepest sense, simply becoming themselves as they are in the intention of God. As the grime of fallen human nature gets wiped away in any person through response to God in faith, not only is the fullness of human potential that is revealed to us in Jesus Christ actualized in that person to some degree. In addition, the world around that person may also be cleansed and become 'natural' once more. In this perspective, 'special' divine providence is inextricably linked to human sanctity, so that it is, for example, no accident that anticipatory experiences of the eschatological state in which 'the wolf will lay down with the lamb' (Isaiah 11:6) are linked in the memory of the Christian community to the response of wild animals to people like Francis of Assisi, Cuthbert of Lindisfarne, and Seraphim of Sarov.[211]

It is in terms of this kind of understanding that we can see the appropriateness of speaking about 'miraculous' events. They are not, for this perspective, the result of supernatural interventions in which the laws of nature are set aside, nor are they manipulations of those laws 'from outside'. They are, rather, what we might call manifestations of 'higher laws of nature' that reflect – more fully than those which are scientifically explorable – God's presence in all things.

This view may not represent any standard exposition of the Orthodox tradition, which hitherto – because of the Orthodox tendency to avoid abstraction – has not felt the need to speak about divine action and miracles in the kind of way that has been usual in the West. Echoes of this view are to be found, nevertheless, in the writings of many Orthodox scholars, and it is arguable that, because of issues arising from the sciences, Orthodoxy does now need to articulate its instincts about these issues more clearly. In particular, it must not only challenge the pretensions to completeness of the kind of naturalism that relates only to the

---

[211] While medieval piety in both East and West often focused on such stories – of which there were many in that period – few Western Christians nowadays remember such stories other than in relation to Francis, who is therefore seen as an anomaly. Orthodox hagiography is still, however, full of comparable tales, even of saints of our own era. See Foltz, *The Noetics of Nature*, 74–5.

sub-natural world of ordinary experience. It must, in addition, explore the possibility of seeing the events usually attributed to 'special divine action' in terms of an 'enhanced naturalism' that reflects the realities of the 'truly natural' world that Christians believe they will experience fully only in the world to come.

My argument in this and the previous two sections has been that a new synthesis may be constructed in which the usual Western distinctions between special and general modes of divine action and between the natural and the supernatural are made redundant. Is this synthesis, we must ask, of interest only to Orthodox? This seems unlikely when we take into account the way in which this approach has been seen, by Sarah Lane Ritchie, as an important component of what she calls a 'theological turn' in twenty-first-century discussion of divine action.[212] This 'turn' is evident for her not only in my own approach but also in the revision of scholastic understandings developed within the Roman Catholic world by Michael Dodds and in the focus on the Holy Spirit developed within the Pentecostal/charismatic strands of the Protestant world by Amos Yong and James Smith.[213]

In relation to the concept of miracles, this latter strand of the 'theological turn' manifests important parallels between the 'incarnational naturalism' of my own approach, based on Orthodox insights, and what Ritchie calls the 'pneumatological naturalism' of Yong and Smith. As we have seen, in my own way of expressing the Orthodox understanding, miraculous events are an aspect of the 'natural' functioning of the world that normally requires human response to God to be activated. In a comparable way, the pneumatological approach is, as Ritchie puts it, one in which the way that 'some events seem more supernatural than others ... is due the varying levels of creaturely response and openness to the Spirit'.[214] Here, she quotes Smith as saying that such events are 'sped-up modes of the Spirit's more regular presences',[215] and this clearly parallels my own view of the way that such events may be seen as the outcome of the presence of the divine *Logos* in both 'lower' and 'higher' laws of nature.

Indeed, since Orthodox perspectives are always Trinitarian, the views of the Protestant pneumatologists are already implicitly present in Orthodox thinking about the presence of this *Logos*. (In the work of the Cappadocian Fathers, for example, divine action is always Trinitarian, and Irenaeus sees the Son and the

---

[212] Ritchie, 'Dancing Around the Causal Joint'. (The insights of this paper have been expanded in an important book: Richie, *Divine Action and the Human Mind*.)

[213] See Dodds, *Unlocking Divine Action*; Yong, *The Spirit of Creation*; Smith, *Thinking in Tongues.*

[214] Ritchie, 'Dancing Around the Causal Joint', 375.

[215] Smith, 'Is the Universe Open for Surprise?', 892.

Spirit as the 'two hands' of the Father.) What Ritchie's analysis of Western pneumatological thinking within the 'theological turn' has made much clearer is that the Orthodox approach that I have presented – with its focus on the divine *Logos* – may be seen as only one aspect of the truly Trinitarian understanding that is intrinsic to Orthodoxy.

The reader of this study who wishes to explore further the 'neo-Byzantine' model of divine action that I have discussed must be referred to the books and papers that I have cited, as well as to the book in which Ritchie analyses the theological turn that she perceives in recent discussions of divine action.[216] As we have already seen in outline, however, this neo-Byzantine model is one in which the occurrence of miraculous events is not to be denied. Equally, however, these events are not to be understood in terms of the kind of naturalism that sees their occurrence as requiring God either to set aside the laws of nature or else to manipulate those laws through some kind of causal joint. In this model, an alternative to such approaches is to be found in a new and 'enhanced' kind of naturalism – an *incarnational naturalism* – based on the way in which, as we have seen in Section 4, Maximus the Confessor interprets the incarnation of the divine *Logos* in terms of the presence of that *Logos* in all created things.

What is envisaged in this understanding is not, it must be emphasized, an extension of the classic deism in which God is envisaged as having, at some point in the past, created the world with certain 'fixed instructions' built into it. Rather, as Ritchie has rightly noted in her analysis of the model I have articulated, the act of creation – incorporating the setting up of the fixed instructions – is not, for this model, 'to be thought of as occurring in the past; to do so is to presume an essentially erroneous relationship between God and time'. One should not, she goes on, think of this setting up 'as occurring in a far distant past – rather it is eternal and being subjectively experienced within temporal constraints'.[217] It is in this way, she explains, that the model is not one in which we are unable to speak of God's personal 'responses' to events in the world. Rather, the model is based on the argument that 'responsiveness should not be conflated with temporality'.[218] (What is envisaged here is in fact based on an expansion – incorporating 'higher laws of nature' – of a very traditional understanding of the origin of the laws of nature. As Thomas Torrance has said of Basil the Great's understanding, 'though acts of divine creation took place timelessly, the creative commands of God gave rise to orderly sequences

---

[216] Ritchie, *Divine Action and the Human Mind* – in which the eighth chapter is devoted to what she calls my 'panentheistic' model. This model – first called 'neo-Byzantine' in Knight, 'Divine Action: A Neo-Byzantine Model' – is also discussed (albeit in a briefer way) in Messer, *Science in Theology*.

[217] Ritchie, *Divine Action and the Human Mind*, 286.   [218] Ibid., 282.

and enduring structures in the world of time and space. It was thus that the voice of God in creation gave rise to laws of nature.')[219]

In much of the science-theology literature, this kind of 'single act' model of divine action is dismissed as inconsistent with basic Christian commitments. Often this is because this model is simplistically identified with Maurice Wiles's version of it, in which miraculous events are regarded as impossible because temporal divine intervention is denied.[220] As we have seen in this section, however, it is possible to question – on both philosophical and theological grounds – Wiles's assumption that the events usually called miraculous can only come about through such intervention. A single-act account, when rooted in a more traditional theological understanding of the kind I have outlined, can be of a quite different kind, in which the central Christian affirmation of the occurrence of events that seem 'above nature' is not regarded as questionable but is actually reinforced.

---

[219] Torrance, *The Christian Frame of Mind*, 4.   [220] Wiles, *God's Action in the World*.

Afterword

My previous book, *Science and the Christian Faith*, was aimed at a different audience from that at which this study has been aimed. One thing common to both that earlier book and this study is, nevertheless, the way in which I have expressed my conviction that Western Christian scholars of the present day tend to have certain blind spots (or at least blurred vision) in their search for a coherent response to theological questions that arise from scientific understanding. In that earlier book, I listed these blind spots under five headings.[221] However, in the context of the different audience intended here, I need to add a sixth in order to reflect what I have said in Section 1. (This is put first in the list that follows.) These blind spots relate to the following aspects of Orthodox thinking:

(1) Its understanding of how philosophy may authentically be used in the theological task
(2) Its understanding of the use and limitations of theological and scientific languages
(3) Its understanding of the role of humanity in bringing God's purposes to fulfilment
(4) Its sense that material entities should be understood less in materialist terms than in relation to the 'mind of God'
(5) Its Christological focus in understanding the concept of creation
(6) Its sense that the empirical world can be understood theologically only when 'the world to come' is taken fully into account.

As we have seen, one of the results of these blind spots has been that many participants in the science-theology dialogue have tended to see science as pointing to a cosmos that consists of an autonomous set of entities and laws that God must manipulate 'from the outside' if His will is to be fulfilled. This has meant that divine action has been seen by many of them as a theological 'problem' that can only be solved by identifying a 'causal joint' through which God can affect the world's processes. However, these participants are slowly becoming aware, through Ritchie's analysis, that a 'theological turn' in discussion of this topic may be necessary.

Implicit in much of what I have written in this study is my belief that this topic of divine action is not the only one that might benefit from a theological turn.

---

[221] Knight, *Science and the Christian Faith*, 35–6.

Often, as we have seen, this need for a theological turn is suggested not only by patristic theological perspectives but also by philosophical considerations that point in a similar direction. I do not claim that the theological turn that I have proposed in these other areas can arise only from the particular way in which Orthodoxy frames the relevant issues. It may well be that – as has happened in discussions of divine action – comparable contributions will prove to be available using Western Christian resources. (Among these resources, I regard the approach that I have noted several times in passing – that of the *nouvelle théologie* developed in the twentieth century within the Roman Catholic world – as perhaps the most promising, not least because of the 'deep appreciation for the Greek Fathers' to be found in many of its developers, which enabled them, as Hans Boersma has rightly noted, 'to counter the neo-scholastic separation between nature and the supernatural with a sacramental ontology'.)[222]

Whatever Western resources prove eventually to be relevant, however, an understanding of Orthodox perspectives can surely still be helpful to us. Even if we do not judge these perspectives in the way that I do – as constituting a persuasive alternative to the pan-Christian vision that has become dominant in the science-theology dialogue – we can still surely see them as providing, at a conceptual level, ways of looking at particular issues that offer new and important insights.

---

[222] Boersma, 'Nature and the Supernatural in *la Nouvelle Théologie*', 46. In this article, Boersma points to aspects of the thinking of Marie-Dominique Chenu – and particularly his focus on the pseudo-Dionysian writings – which arguably bring Chenu particularly close to the Orthodox understanding I have set out.

Bibliographies

Further Reading

Buxhoeveden, Daniel, and Woloschak, Gayle, eds., *Science and the Eastern Orthodox Church* (Farnham, UK: Ashgate, 2011)

Dragas, George D., Pavolov, Pavel, and Tanev, Stoyan, eds., *Orthodox Theology and the Sciences: Glorifying God in His Marvelous Works* (Columbia, MO: New Rome Press, 2016)

Knight, Christopher C., and Nesteruk, Alexei V., eds., *Eastern Orthodox Christianity and the Sciences: Theological, Philosophical and Scientific Aspects of the Dialogue* (Turnhout: Brepols, 2021)

Theokritoff, Elizabeth, and Knight, Christopher C., '20th and 21st Century Orthodox Voices on Nature and Science', in *T&T Clark Handbook of Christian Theology and The Modern Sciences*, ed. John P. Slattery (London: T&T Clark, 2020) 177–90

Woloschak, Gayle E., and Makrides, Vasilios N., eds., *Orthodox Christianity and Modern Science: Tensions, Ambiguities, Potential* (Turnhout: Brepols, 2019)

Bibliography

Alston, William P., *Perceiving God: The Epistemology of Religious Experience* (Ithaca, NY: Cornell University Press, 1991)

Amis, Robin, *A Different Christianity: Early Christian Esotericism and Modern Thought* (Albany: State University of New York, 1985)

Atmanspacher, Harald, 'The Pauli-Jung Conjecture and Its Relatives: A Formally Augmented Outline', *Open Philosophy*, www.degruyter.com/document/doi/10.1515/opphil-2020-0138/html

Ayer, A. J., *Language, Truth and Logic* (London: Gollancz, 1946)

Barbour, Ian G., *Issues in Science and Religion* (London: SCM, 1966)

Barbour, Ian G., *Religion in an Age of Science: The Gifford Lectures 1989–1991*, Vol. 1 (London: SCM, 1990)

Barrow, John D., and Tipler, Frank J., *The Anthropic Cosmological Principle* (Oxford: Clarendon, 1986)

Berger, Peter, *A Rumour of Angels: Modern Society and the Rediscovery of the Supernatural* (Harmondsworth: Penguin, 1969)

Bird, Alexander, and Tobin, Emma, 'Natural Kinds', *The Stanford Encyclopedia of Philosophy*, ed. Edward N. Zalta (2018), https://plato.stanford.edu/archives/spr2018/entries/natural-kinds/

Blowers, Paul, *Maximus the Confessor: Jesus Christ and the Transfiguration of the World* (Oxford: Oxford University Press, 2016)

Boersma, Hans, 'Nature and the Supernatural in *la nouvelle théologie*: The Recovery of a Sacramental Mindset', *New Blackfriars* 93 (2012) 34–46

Boersma, Hans, *Nouvelle Théologie and Sacramental Ontology: A Return to Mystery* (Oxford: Oxford University Press, 2009)

Bohm, David, *Wholeness and the Implicate Order* (London: Routledge and Kegan Paul, 1980)

Bradshaw, David, 'Introduction', in *Natural Theology in the Eastern Orthodox Tradition*, ed. David Bradshaw and Richard Swinburne (St.Paul, MN: IOTA, 2021) 1–21

Bradshaw, David, 'The Logoi of Beings in Patristic Thought', in *Toward an Ecology of Transfiguration: Orthodox Christian Perspectives on Environment, Nature, and Creation*, ed. Bruce Foltz and John Chryssavgis (New York: Fordham University Press, 2013) 9-22

Bradshaw, David, 'The Mind and the Heart in Christian East and West', *Faith and Philosophy* 26 (2009) 576–98

Bradshaw, David, and Swinburne, Richard, eds., *Natural Theology in the Eastern Orthodox Tradition* (St. Paul, MN: IOTA, 2021)

Brent, James, 'Natural Theology', *Internet Encyclopedia of Philosophy* (2020), https://iep.utm.edu/theo-nat/#H5

Brown, Warren S., and Strawn, Brad. D., *The Physical Nature of Christian Life: Neuroscience, Psychology and the Church* (Cambridge: Cambridge University Press, 2012)

Bulgakov, Sergius, *Bride of the Lamb* (Grand Rapids, MI: Eerdmans, 2002)

Ceglie, Roberto di, 'Faith, Reason and Charity in Thomas Aquinas's Thought', *International Journal for Philosophy of Religion* 79 (2016) 133–46

Chenoweth, Mark, 'A Maximian Framework for Understanding Evolution', *St Vladimir's Theological Quarterly* 64 (2020) 157–80

Clayton, Philip, 'Panentheism in Metaphysical and Scientific Perspective', in *In Whom We Live and Move and Have Our Being: Panentheistic Reflections on God's Presence in a Scientific World*, ed. Philip Clayton and Arthur Peacocke (Grand Rapids, MI: Eerdmans, 2002) 75–84

Clayton, Philip, and Davies, Paul, eds. *The Re-emergence of Emergence: The Emergentist Hypothesis from Science to Religion* (Oxford: Oxford University Press, 2006)

Clayton, Philip, and Peacocke, Arthur, eds., *In Whom We Live and Move and Have Our Being: Panentheistic Reflections on God's Presence in a Scientific World* (Grand Rapids, MI: Eerdmans, 2002)

Constantine, Theophanes, *The Orthodox Doctrine of the Person*, 2nd ed. (Edmonton: Timios Prodromis, 2014)

Conway Morris, Simon, *Life's Solution: Inevitable Humans in a Lonely Universe* (Cambridge: Cambridge University Press, 2003)

Cooper, Adam G., *The Body in St. Maximus the Confessor: Holy Flesh, Wholly Deified* (Oxford: Oxford University Press, 2005)

Costache, Doru, 'The Orthodox Doctrine of Creation in the Age of Science', *Journal of Orthodox Christian Studies* 2 (2019) 43–64

Darg, Daniel W., 'Cosmic If-Statements', in *God and the Scientist: Exploring the Work of John Polkinghorne*, ed. Fraser Watts and Christopher C. Knight (Farnham, UK: Ashgate, 2012) 93–125

Dawkins, Richard, *The Ancestor's Tale: A Pilgrimage to the Dawn of Life* (London: Weidenfeld and Nicolson, 2004)

Dawkins, Richard, *The Blind Watchmaker: Why the Evidence of Evolution Reveals a Universe without Design* (London: Longman, 1986)

Deane-Drummond, Celia E., *Creation through Wisdom: Theology and the New Biology* (Edinburgh: T & T Clark, 2000)

Dodds, Michael, *Unlocking Divine Action: Contemporary Science and Thomas Aquinas* (Washington, DC: Catholic University of America Press, 2012)

Florovsky, Georges, 'The Ethos of the Orthodox Church', *Ecumenical Review* 12 (1960) 183–98

Flynn, Gabriel, and Murray, Paul D., *Resourcement: A Movement for Renewal in Twentieth-Century Catholic Theology* (Oxford: Oxford University Press, 2011)

Foltz, Bruce V., *The Noetics of Nature: Environmental Philosophy and the Holy Beauty of the Visible* (New York: Fordham University Press, 2014)

Goldstein, Sheldon, 'Bohmian Mechanics', *The Stanford Encyclopedia of Philosophy*, ed. Edward N. Zalta (2021), https://plato.stanford.edu/archives/fall2021/entries/qm-bohm/

Gould, Stephen Jay, 'Nonoverlapping Magisteria', *Natural History* 106 (1997) 16–22

Harré, Rom, *Varieties of Realism: A Rationale for the Natural Sciences* (Oxford: Basil Blackwell, 1986)

Harrison, Peter, *The Fall of Man and the Foundations of Science* (Cambridge: Cambridge University Press, 2007)

Haught, John F., *God after Darwin: A Theology of Evolution* (Boulder, CO: Westview, 2000)

Henn, W., *The Hierarchy of Truths According to Yves Congar. O.P.*, Analecta Gregoriana 246 (Rome, Analecta Gregoriana, 1987)

Hesse, M. B., 'Physics, Philosophy and Myth', in *Physics, Philosophy and Theology: A Common Quest for Understanding*, ed. R. J. Russell, W. R. Stoeger, and G. V. Coyne (Vatican City State: Vatican Observatory, 1988)185–99

Hibbs, Darren, 'Was Gregory of Nyssa a Berkeleyan Idealist?', *British Journal of Philosophy* 13 (2005) 425–35

Hick, John, *Evil and the God of Love* (London: Collins, 1966)

Hick, John, *An Interpretation of Religion: Human Responses to the Transcendent* (New Haven, CT: Yale University Press, 1989)

Hill, Jonathan, 'Gregory of Nyssa, Material Substance and Berkeleyan Idealism', *British Journal of Philosophy* 17 (2009) 653–83

Huyssteen, J. Wentzel van, 'Postfoundationalism in Theology and Science', in *Rethinking Theology and Science: Six Models for the Current Dialogue*, ed. Niels Henrik Gregersen and J. Wentzel van Huyssteen (Grand Rapids, MI: Eerdmans, 1998) 13–49

Jeans, James, *The Mysterious Universe* (Cambridge: Cambridge University Press, 1930)

Karamanolis, George, *The Philosophy of Early Christianity* (Durham: Acumen, 2013)

Knight, Christopher C., '"Analytic" Natural Theology: Orthodox or Otherwise?', *St Vladimir's Theological Quarterly* 65 (2021) 57–85

Knight, Christopher C., 'An Apophatic Approach to God's "Personal" Nature', in *The Divine Nature: Personal and A-personal Perspectives*, ed. Simon Kittle and Georg Gasser (London: Routledge, 2022) 195–212

Knight, Christopher C., 'Astrobiology and Theology: Uneasy Partners?', in *The History and Philosophy of Astrobiology: Perspectives on Extraterrestrial Life and the Human Mind*, ed. David Duner (Newcastle upon Tyne: Cambridge Scholars, 2013) 245–56

Knight, Christopher C., 'Divine Action: A Neo-Byzantine Model', *International Journal for Philosophy of Religion* 58 (2005) 181–99

Knight, Christopher C., *The God of Nature: Incarnation and Contemporary Science* (Minneapolis, MN: Fortress, 2007)

Knight, Christopher C., 'Natural Theology: Complementary Perspectives from the Science-Theology Dialogue and the Eastern Orthodox Tradition', *Philosophy, Theology and the Sciences* 8 (2021) 259–284

Knight, Christopher C., 'Natural Theology and the Eastern Orthodox Tradition', in *The Oxford Handbook of Natural Theology, ed. Russell Re Manning* (Oxford: Oxford University Press, 2013), 213–26

Knight, Christopher C., *Science and the Christian Faith: A Guide for the Perplexed* (Yonkers, NY: St Vladimir's Seminary Press, 2020)

Knight, Christopher C., 'Theistic Naturalism and the Word Made Flesh: Complementary Approaches to the Debate on Panentheism', in *In Whom We Live and Move and Have Our Being: Panentheistic Reflections on God's Presence in a Scientific World*, ed. Philip Clayton and Arthur Peacocke (Grand Rapids, MI: Eerdmans, 2002)

Knight, Christopher C., *Wrestling with the Divine: Science, Religion, and Revelation* (Minneapolis, MN: Fortress, 2001)

Knight, George T., 'The Definition of the Supernatural', *Harvard Theological Review* 3 (1910) 310–24

Kuhn, Thomas S., *The Structure of Scientific Revolutions* (Chicago: University of Chicago Press, 1962)

Ladouceur, Paul, 'Evolution and Genesis 2–3: The Decline and Fall of Adam and Eve', *St Vladimir's Theological Quarterly* 57 (2013)

Laird Martin, *Gregory of Nyssa and the Grasp of Faith: Union, Knowledge and Divine Presence* (Oxford: Oxford University Press, 2004)

Liston, Michael, 'Scientific Realism and Antirealism', *Internet Encyclopedia of Philosophy* (n.d.), https://iep.utm.edu/sci-real/

Lollar, Joshua, *To See into the Life of Things: The Contemplation of Nature in Maximus the Confessor and His Predecessors* (Turnhout: Brepols, 2013)

Lossky, Vladimir, *The Mystical Theology of the Eastern Church* (Cambridge: James Clarke, 1957)

Loudovikos, Nikolaos, *A Eucharistic Ontology: Maximus the Confessor's Eschatological Ontology* (Brookline, MA: Holy Cross, 2010)

Louth, Andrew, *Introducing Eastern Orthodoxy* (London: SPCK, 2013)

Louth, Andrew, *Maximus the Confessor* (London: Routledge, 1996)

Lucas, J. R. 'The Temporality of God', in *Quantum Cosmology and the Laws of Nature: Scientific Perspectives on Divine Action*, ed. Robert John Russell, Nancey Murphey, and C. J. Isham (Vatican City State: Vatical Observatory, 1993) 235–46

Manning, Russell Re, ed., *The Oxford Handbook of Natural Theology* (Oxford: Oxford University Press, 2013)

McGrath, Alister, *The Open Secret: A New Vision for Natural Theology* (Oxford: Blackwell, 2008)

McGrath, Alister, *Thomas F. Torrance: An Intellectual Biography* (Edinburgh: T & T Clark, 1999)

McInerny, Ralph, *Praeambula Fidei: Thomism and the God of the Philosophers* (Washington, DC: Catholic University of America Press, 2006)

Messer, Niel, *Science in Theology: Encounters Between Science and the Christian Tradition* (London: T & T Clark, 2020)

Moore, Andrew, 'Theological Critiques of Natural Theology', in *The Oxford Handbook of Natural Theology*, ed. Russell Re Manning (Oxford: Oxford University Press, 2013) 227–44

Moore, Aubrey L., *Science and Faith* (London: Kegan Paul, Trench and Co., 1889)

Moroney, Stephen K., *The Noetic Effects of Sin: An Historical and Contemporary Exploration of How Sin Affects Our Thinking* (Lanham, MD: Lexington Books, 2000)

Murphy, Nancey, *Bodies and Souls, or Spirited Bodies?* (Cambridge: Cambridge University Press, 2006)

Need, Stephen W., 'Re-reading the Prologue: Incarnation and Creation in John 1: 1–18', *Theology* 106 (2003) 397–404

Nellas, Panayiotis, *Deification in Christ: The Nature of the Human Person* (Crestwood, NY: St Vladimir's Seminary Press, 1997)

Nesteruk, Alexei, *The Universe As Communion: Towards a Neo-Patristic Synthesis of Theology and Science* (London: T & T Clark, 2008)

Newberg, Andrew, *Principles of Neurotheology* (Farnham: Ashgate, 2010)

Nicolaidis, Efthymios, *Science and Eastern Orthodoxy: From the Greek Fathers to the Age of Globalization* (Baltimore, MD: Johns Hopkins University Press, 2011)

Nicolescu, Basarab, *Manifesto of Transdisciplinarity* (New York: State University Press of New York, 2002)

Oaley, Francis, 'Christian Theology and the Newtonian Science: The Rise of the Concept of Laws of Nature', *Church History* 30 (1961) 433–57

Oddie, Graham, 'Truthlikeness', *The Stanford Encyclopedia of Philosophy*, ed. Edward N. Zalta (2016), https://plato.stanford.edu/archives/win2016/entries/truthlikeness/

Oppy, Graham, 'Arguments for Atheism', in *The Oxford Handbook of Atheism*, ed. Stephen Bullivant and Michael Ruse (Oxford: Oxford University Press, 2013) 53–70

Palmer, G. E. H., Sherrard, Philip, and Ware, Kallistos, eds. *The Philokalia*, Vol. 1 (London: Faber and Faber, 1979)

Pannenberg, Wolfhart, 'The Concept of Miracle', *Zygon: Journal of Religion and Science* 37 (2002) 759–62

Peacocke, Arthur R., 'God's Interaction with the World: The Implications of Deterministic "Chaos" and of Interconnected and Interdependent Complexity', in *Chaos and Complexity: Scientific Perspectives on Divine Action*, ed. Robert John Russell, Nancey Murphy, and Arthur R. Peacocke (Vatican City State: Vatican Observatory, 1995) 263–87

Peacocke, Arthur, *Intimations of Reality: Critical Realism in Science and Theology* (Notre Dame, IN: University of Notre Dame Press, 1984)

Peacocke, Arthur, _Paths from Science towards God: The End of All Our Exploring_ (London: Oneworld, 2001)

Penrose, Roger, _The Emperor's New Mind: Concerning Computers, Minds, and the Laws of Physics_ (Oxford: Oxford University Press, 1989)

Polkinghorne, John, _Beyond Science: The Wider Human Context_ (Cambridge: Cambridge University Press, 1996)

Polkinghorne, John, _Faith, Science and Understanding_ (London: SPCK, 2000)

Polkinghorne, John, _One World : The Interaction of Science and Theology_ (London: SPCK, 1986)

Polkinghorne, John, 'The Person, the Soul, and Genetic Engineering', _Journal of Medical Ethics_ 30 (2004) 593–7

Polkinghorne, John, _Reason and Reality: The Relationship Between Science and Theology_ (London: SPCK, 1991)

Polkinghorne, John, _Science and Christian Belief: Theological Reflections of a Bottom-Up Thinker_ (London: SPCK, 1994)

Polkinghorne, John, _Science and Creation: The Search for Understanding_ (London: SPCK, 1988)

Polkinghorne, John, _Scientists As Theologians: A Comparison of the Writings of Ian Barbour, Arthur Peacocke, and John Polkinghorne_ (London: SPCK, 1996)

Polkinghorne, John C., _The Quantum World_ (Princeton, NJ: Princeton University Press, 1985)

Pollard, W. G., _Chance and Providence_ (London: Faber and Faber, 1958)

Puhalo, Lazar, _On the Neurobiology of Sin_ (Dewdney, BC: Synaxis, 2010)

Quine, W. V., 'Ontological Relativity', in _Ontological Relativity and Other Essays_ (New York: Columbia University Press, 1969) 26–68

Ritchie, Sarah Lane, 'Dancing Around the Causal Joint: Challenging The Theological Turn in Divine Action Theories', _Zygon: Journal of Religion and Science_ 37 (2017) 362–79

Ritchie, Sarah Lane, _Divine Action and the Human Mind_ (Cambridge: Cambridge University Press, 2019)

Rose, Seraphim, _Genesis, Creation, and Early Man_ (Platina, CA: St Herman of Alaska Brotherhood, 2000)

Russell, Robert John, 'Bodily Resurrection, Eschatology, and Scientific Cosmology', in _Resurrection: Theological and Scientific Assessments_, ed. Ted Peters, Robert John Russell, and Michael Welker (Grand Rapids, MI: Eerdmans, 2002) 3–30

Saunders, Nicholas, _Divine Action and Modern Science_ (Cambridge: Cambridge University Press, 2002)

Schmemann, Alexander, *The Eucharist: Sacrament of the Kingdom* (Crestwood, NY: St Vladimir's Seminary Press, 1987)

Schooping, Joshua, 'Touching the Mind of God: Patristic Christian Thought on the Nature of Matter', *Zygon: Journal of Religion and Science* 50 (2015) 583–603

Schwartz, Stephen P., *Naming, Necessity, and Natural Kinds* (Ithaca, NY: Cornell University Press, 1973)

Sherrard, Philip, *Christianity and Eros: Essays on the Theme of Sexual Love* (London: SPCK, 1976)

Sherrard, Philip, *Christianity: Lineaments of a Sacred Tradition* (Edinburgh: T & T Clark, 1998)

Sherrard, Philip, 'The Sacrament', in *The Orthodox Ethos: Essays in Honour of the Centenary of the Greek Orthodox Archdiocese of North and South America*, Vol. 1, ed. A. J. Philippou (Oxford: Holywell Press, 1964)

Silva, Ignacio, 'Divine Action and Thomism: Why Thomas Aquinas's Thought Is Attractive Today', *Acta Philosophica* 25 (2016) 65–84

Smith, James A. K., 'Is the Universe Open for Surprise? Pentecostal Ontology and the Spirit of Naturalism', *Zygon: Journal of Religion and Science* 43 (2008) 879–96

Smith, James A. K., *Thinking in Tongues: Pentecostal Contributions to Christian Philosophy* (Grand Rapids, MI: Eerdmans, 2010)

Soskice, Janet Martin, *Metaphor and Religious Language* (Oxford: Clarendon, 1985)

Swafford, Andrew Dean, *Nature and Grace: A New Approach to Thomistic Resourcement* (Cambridge: James Clarke, 2014)

Swinburne, Richard, *The Existence of God*, 2nd ed. (Oxford: Oxford University Press, 2004)

Tanev, Stoyan, *Energy in Orthodox Theology and Physics: From Controversy to Encounter* (Eugene, OR: Pickwick, 2017)

Theokritoff, Elizabeth, 'Creator and Creation', in *The Cambridge Companion to Orthodox Christian Theology*, ed. Mary B. Cunningham and Elizabeth Theokritoff (Cambridge: Cambridge University Press, 2008)

Thunberg, Lars, *Man and the Cosmos: The Vision of Saint Maximus the Confessor* (Crestwood, NY: St Vladimir's Seminary Press, 1985)

Thunberg, Lars, *Microcosm and Mediator: The Theological Anthropology of Maximus the Confessor* (Chicago, IL: Open Court, 1995)

Till, Howard van, 'Basil, Augustine, and the Doctrine of Creation's Functional Integrity', *Science and Christian Belief* 8 (1996) 21–38

Torrance, Thomas F., *The Christian Frame of Mind* (Colorado Springs, CO: Helmers and Howard, 1989)

Torrance, Thomas F., *Reality and Scientific Theology* (Edinburgh: Scottish Academic Press, 1985)

Uleman, James S., 'Introduction: Becoming Aware of the New Unconscious', in *The New Unconscious*, ed. Ran R. Hassin, James S. Uleman, and John A. Barr (Oxford: Oxford University Press, 2005) 3–18

Von Balthasar, Hans Urs, *Cosmic Liturgy: The Universe According to Maximus the Confessor*, 3rd ed. (San Francisco, CA: Ignatius, 1993)

Vujisic, Zoran, *The Art and Science of Healing the Soul: A Guide to Orthodox Psychotherapy* (Saarbrucken: VDM Verlag Dr. Muller, 2010)

Ward, Keith, 'Bishop Berkeley's Castle: John Polkinghorne on the Soul', in *God and the Scientist: Exploring the Work of John Polkinghorne*, ed. Fraser Watts and Christopher C. Knight (Farnham: Ashgate, 2012) 127–37

Ward, Keith, *More Than Matter: What Humans Really Are* (Oxford: Lion Hudson, 2010)

Ware, Kallistos, Bishop of Diokleia, 'God Immanent Yet Transcendent: The Divine Energies According to Saint Gregory Palamas', in *In Whom We Live and Move and Have Our Being: Panentheistic Reflections on God's Presence in a Scientific World*, ed. Philip Clayton and Arthur Peacocke (Grand Rapids, MI: Eerdmans, 2002) 157–68

Ware, Timothy, *The Orthodox Church* (Harmondsworth: Penguin, 1963)

Whitehead, A. N., *Science and the Modern World* (New York: Mentor Books, 1948)

Wildman, Wesley, 'The Divine Action Project, 1988 to 2003', *Theology and Science* 2 (2010) 31–75

Wildman, Wesley, 'Robert John Russell's Theology of God's Action', in *God's Action in the World: Essays in Honour of Robert John Russell*, ed. Ted Peters and Nathan Hallanger (Aldershot: Ashgate, 2006) 147–70

Wiles, Maurice, *God's Action in the World: The Bampton Lectures for 1986* (London: SCM, 1986)

Wilson, Robert A., and Foglia, Lucia, 'Embodied Cognition', *The Stanford Encyclopedia of Philosophy*, ed. Edward N. Zalta (2017), https://plato.stan ford.edu/archives/spr2017/entries/embodied-cognition/

Woloschak, Gayle E., *Faith, Science, Mystery* (Alhambra: Sebastien, 2018)

Yannaras, Christos, *The Enigma of Evil* (Brookline, MA: Holy Cross, 2012)

Yannaras, Christos, *Postmodern Metaphysics*, tr. Norman Russell (Brookline, MA: Holy Cross, 2005)

Yong, Amos, *The Spirit of Creation: Modern Science and Divine Action in the Pentecostal-Charismatic Imagination* (Grand Rapids, MI: Eerdmans, 2011)

About the Author

For the ten years before his retirement, Christopher C. Knight was the Executive Secretary of the International Society for Science and Religion. Before entering the Eastern Orthodox Church, in which he is now a priest, he had served as an Anglican priest in several posts, the last of which was Chaplain, Fellow, and Director of Studies in Theology at Sidney Sussex College, Cambridge. He is now a Senior Research Associate of the Institute for Orthodox Christian Studies in Cambridge and is the author of numerous papers on the science-theology dialogue as well as three full-length books: *Wrestling With the Divine: Religion, Science, and Revelation* (2001), *The God of Nature: Incarnation and Contemporary Science* (2007) and *Science and the Christian Faith: A Guide for the Perplexed* (2020).

Acknowledgements

This publication has been produced within the framework of the project 'Science and Orthodoxy around the World' (SOW), which has been made possible through the support of a grant from the Templeton World Charity Foundation, Inc. The opinions expressed in this publication are those of the author and do not necessarily reflect the views of Project SOW or the Foundation.

Cambridge Elements ☰

Christianity and Science

Andrew Davison
University of Cambridge

Andrew Davison is the Starbridge Associate Professor in Theology and Science at the University of Cambridge. He is Fellow of Corpus Christi College and Dean of the Chapel, and oversee the arts and humanities work of the Leverhulme Centre for Life in the Universe at the University of Cambridge.

About the Series
This Elements series on Christianity and science will offer an authoritative presentation of scholarship in this interdisciplinary field of inquiry. Opening new avenues for study and research, the series will highlight several issues, notably: the importance of historical scholarship for understanding the relationship between Christianity and natural science.

Cambridge Elements $\overline{\overline{}}$

Christianity and Science

Elements in the Series

Eastern Orthodoxy and the Science-Theology Dialogue
Christopher C. Knight

A full series listing is available at: www.cambridge.org/EOCS

Printed in the United States
by Baker & Taylor Publisher Services